URBAN IONA

URBAN IONA

Celtic Hospitality in the City

KURT NEILSON

MOREHOUSE PUBLISHING

Morehouse Publishing, PO Box 1321, Harrisburg, PA 17105
Morehouse Publishing, 445 Fifth Avenue, New York, NY 10016
Morehouse Publishing is an imprint of Church Publishing Incorporated

Cover art courtesy of Fotosearch
Cover design by Laurie Klein Westhafer
Interior design by John Eagleson

Library of Congress Cataloging-in-Publication Data

Neilson, Kurt.
    Urban Iona : Celtic hospitality in the city / Kurt Neilson.
        p. cm.
    ISBN 978-0-8192-2234-3 (pbk.)
        1. Christian pilgrims and pilgrimages – Ireland. 2. Ireland – Religious life and customs. 3. Celtic Church – History. 4. Neilson, Kurt. I. Title.
    BX2320.5.I73N45 2007
    263′.042415 – dc22

                                                                    2006038057

Printed in the United States of America

07 08 09 10 11 12   6 5 4 3 2 1

contents

acknowledgments

I RISK MUCH in singling out folks to thank. This book is the result of great faith and great support on the part of many, and the collective dreams and visions of many as well.

I thank my wife, Diane, who shocked me in the midst of our making-ends-meet-life by saying, "I think that if you get the chance to go to Ireland, you should just go." Greater love hath no woman. I thank my kids, Jake, Bridget, and Helen, who did a great job of handling the house and helping Mom while Dad messed around overseas.

I thank the people of Saints Peter and Paul, living, deceased, and departed, who supported me with gifts and prayers. I thank them because after I returned they decided to continue this voyage with me with great faith and trust. And they have been patient with me these many months, cutting me some slack because "Father's doing his writing."

I thank the Companions of Columba and the Culdees for soul-friendship these several years.

I thank now-retired Bishop Robert Ladehoff for the support that made my pilgrimage possible. I thank now-Bishop Johncy Itty and the "folks at the Close" for their ongoing support of the Columba Center's ministries. I thank my clergy sisters and brothers of the Canterbury Way, who manage to be very Celtic while striving to be very Benedictine.

I thank executive editor Nancy Fitzgerald, who answered a letter from an aspiring writer with an unexpected phone call and said, "I think you should write this book."

And I thank those many friends and fellow pilgrims who have chosen to share this vision, who live and work beyond the old "bounds" of parish membership and the blessed "usual suspects." May our borders become ever more porous. May many more affiliate with the *familia* of those whose souls are kindled with the flame of Love which never ceases.

And I thank Bridie and Patrick and baby Thomas. If they were ever lost, may they be found in the love of the Three.

Columba's Rock

Delightful it is to stand on the peak of a rock, in the bosom of the isle,
gazing on the face of the sea.

I hear the heaving waves chanting a tune to God in heaven,
I see their glittering surf. I see the golden beaches, the sands sparkling,
I hear the joyous shrieks of the swooping gulls.

I hear the waves breaking, crashing on rocks, like thunder in heaven.
I see the mighty whales.

I watch the ebb and flow of the ocean tide; it holds my secret,
my mournful flight from Eire.

Contrition fills my heart as I hear the sea; it chants my sins,
sins too numerous to confess.

Let me bless Almighty God, whose power extends over sea and land,
whose angels watch over all.

Let me study sacred books to calm my soul;
I pray for peace, kneeling at heaven's gates.

Let me do my daily work, gathering seaweed, catching fish,
giving food to the poor.

Let me say my daily prayers, sometimes chanting, sometimes quiet,
always thanking God.

Delightful it is to live on a peaceful isle, in a quiet cell,
serving the King of kings.

— *Attributed to Saint Columba*

chapter 1

pilgrim regress

tHIS IS THE STORY of a pilgrimage to the holy places of Ireland and the ancient Celtic isles. But in preparing for pilgrimage, I learned that the journey had begun far earlier than the boarding of a plane with a few pathetic bits of things in secondhand luggage. It began with my birth, and before that with my mother's family's long journey and sorrow coming from dirt-poor Ireland, Ireland with her grand dreams and her grander harsh and deathly realities. And it began properly long before that, when old Celtic faith spoken to the lowering dark and to the wild wind blowing on desolate coast or in twilight oak groves met new faith, the White Christ from the distant South and the Gospel's hope and the stern words of prophets. And in that uneasy alchemy, the place where one people's shadow and soul met the shadow and soul of the desert God of the Hebrews, was born and grew a new faith, a new way of walking with the one God who is Three, the triune God who is One.

And the end? Is there one, a proper end, so that one may move on to something wholly different, fresh start, clean slate? I don't think so. I write because I have not as yet come back. Even sitting comfortably with the last of the morning's coffee with the cherished summer sunlight of western Oregon warm on the keyboard, I have not come back. The journey gave birth to a restless vision, a way of living faith and service passionately in the desert of contemporary America. I've been a lifelong pilgrim, willing to learn from all people of goodwill and good faith, people who possess the indefinite air of lingering conversation with the Divine. I feel more than ever that to be a person of faith and thought and honesty is to walk a faint desert track. The track winds between rocks and stones and shifting quicksand. On one side are those who claim the voice of

1

God for themselves, the Pharisees of our time. Were I not acculturated to traditional Christianity, I think I might not have anything to do with the Christ who is proclaimed with marketing deftness in today's U.S.A. There's little that is attractive to me about a faith which presents itself as pro-war, indifferent to poverty and injustice, and selectively literal in its use of the Bible to justify its politics and prejudices. In my own house, my articulate son says to his friends that he is "the other kind of Christian," when his friends assume that he and we must espouse the most vocal face of Christianity today.

But my bashing of the "benighted" folks makes me into the same sort of judgmental creature, the flip side of the same coin. I am as sick of my own judgmental rant as I am of the culture and religious wars of our era. It is all so self-referential and so deeply unattractive to honest people who might otherwise explore New Testament faith. Part of the desert journey of faith these days is to walk amidst the thorns and stones of one's own self-righteousness. I've grown weary of fighting for the moral high ground, either looking up at those who have taken it or trying to scrabble to the top myself. We give up playing "king of the hill," as it is unending, and only children have the energy to keep playing and the wisdom to know that it is in the end only a silly game.

But we are still addressed, we are still spoken to and loved by the One who spoke so long ago, who spoke with words of love and hope and a vision of an earth and a humanity renewed, living whole and healed and at peace and empowered to speak the unspeakable Word in our words and by our lives. That's why there's hope and that's why this conversation is worth having and that's why there is still a pilgrim road to walk today.

I still have the cheap brown backpack I took with me on my journey. It now holds my tae kwon do black belt, another pilgrim token. The backpack rode across the Atlantic, through London Heathrow with its twisted little hallways labeled "remodeled," to Glasgow in Scotland, blunt and hearty town, an acquired taste like a good Scotch whiskey.

The pack rode, swollen and silent, on a train rack through the fabled Scottish Highlands and the last forlorn remnants of the Caledonian Forest to a ferry port guarded by castles. It held a leftover prawn sandwich and sat patiently on a ferry floor, was hid away in a bus's belly across sheep-strewn roads on the Isle of Mull. It held a pilgrim's journal and a book of peoples' prayers to the ancient holy stones of Iona, Columba's isle, heart of the northern seas. The backpack's dark brown skin drank cold Scottish rain, doubling its weight, and went the distance through driving storm along the medieval pilgrim's path to Columba's Bay and the holy cairns of stones raised when Saxons fought Britons and Rome burned and druids cried their chants at the waning of the moon. The pack rode in the trunk of a car along the Falls Road in Belfast, where blood was shed by bomb and gun, where the beautiful, deathly murals bid Catholic slay Protestant and Protestant slay Catholic in the name of Christ and country and blood and the heroes of old Ireland.

The backpack heard Evensong's chant and pub's hubbub, smelled wax melted in prayer, looked over endless waters at a saint's chosen solitude. It leaned on holy stones made smooth by monk's hands and pilgrims' lips. Finally, it was cast down in the soft and sweet grass, green as hope and wet with dew, at the holiest well of holy Ireland while its owner, reserved white guy with a beard, sobbed as he'd never sobbed before, placed all his prayers and soul into a saint's well and waited, empty and lost, for the mercy of God.

It has come through water and fire and faith and doubt and desolation and war and devil's twisted wish and God's clear promise. It has come home. But I have not. Iona still haunts my dreams. I wonder now as I have wondered before in a pilgrim life: where is home? Writing these words, I wonder if that question has become its own answer.

I need to tell this tale, to search my word-hoard for the right maps to show the road to any who wish to walk it. The road led to Columba's lonely island and to Ireland's green, wet hillsides. The road has also led to my becoming a middle-class, postmodern religious tramp, neither tourist nor sage. It has led to a vision put into words and action for a parish community, a church, transforming some and calling others to be pilgrims as well. The journey continues as I write, and I see no ending that I can put into words. Tolkien's hobbits sang, "The road goes ever on. . . . " I thank you for reading and so sharing a pilgrim's road with me. It's a long journey, and we all need the help and the joy of companions.

May the God of Goings and journey's end walk with us and bring us to our "place of resurrection," which the ancient Celtic Christians sought by boat and foot, and in heart and mind. Above all, we must hold in trust that we have not been lied to — that our heart's deep longing and the hope of the world will be slaked before the end.

chapter 2

the pilgrim

I'm FORTY-EIGHT, a middle-aged white guy. Some gray in the beard, but as the prophet Jerry Garcia sang, "O wear the touch of gray; kinda suits you anyway. . . . " The touch of gray fools people into thinking that I may be wise. So long as I keep quiet and nod meaningfully they keep on thinking so. I'm beginning to not care about the "gotta do's" and "shoulds" that seemed so important in my early decades. Although I hear fewer divine "shoulds," the God who got the blame as the should-generator seems more real these days — a different God who is unresolved and filled with divine ambiguity. I feel less and less need to have all the pieces of life and truth and faith hang together neatly. There is less to prove these days and I like that. I recommend the forties to you, although it is too bad about the wrinkles and the whole mortality thing.

Mid-life is enough to send most of us on some kind of pilgrimage. Pilgrim records show that indeed middle-age tends to be the season of pilgrimage, as life obligations ease yet one has enough energy for a journey. One hears the road-song, seductive and persistent. In my case, the pilgrimage was spoken into being in me by stories.

I blame my mother. Mom and Dad were both Depression-era kids, uprooted souls, both by birth as well as by the economic apocalypse of 1930s U.S.A. Dad was part Tlingit Indian on his mother's side, first-generation Danish on his father's. His tough-minded Tlingit mother walked out on his Danish tinker dad, and she boarded out dad and his sister while she worked at various things. If he was an uprooted soul, Mom was too. Mom was first-generation Irish-American, orphaned and left without a sibling through the slashing misery of the TB and cholera epidemics that ravaged the ethnic ghettos of early-twentieth-century New York. She was raised by cousins of a side of the family who thoroughly disapproved of her parents and their forbidden marriage. She was told that they were bad people and not to be remembered, and although folks doted on "little Peggy," as they called her, Mom never lost a sense of being alone for the whole of her long life.

It is a sin to tell a person not to remember.

Dad and Mom married after Dad wrote a stack of innocently torrid love letters which I still have. An iron-fisted old Irish priest refused to marry the "nice Catholic girl" to a Protestant, so the assistant priest played good cop and married them privately in the rectory parlor. They lived for six months on Mom's cousins' couch. After a few years, Dad brought his Irish Catholic Democrat bride with labor-union sympathies to WASP Long Island, where she and their three kids, one on the way, stuck out like sore thumbs. From stem to stern, Dad and Mom understood what it meant to be strangers, aliens, with no permanent home except the one they made for themselves by Dad working jobs he never really liked and Mom slaving in the house, cleaning up after six noisy and innocently violent sons. They saw the stranger in one another, I believe. Strange how our wounds attract one another, how we gravitate to those whose lives echo our own chief wound and question.

We were raised on stories because Mom was a born storyteller. Irish folk understand the world and their own lives through story, speaking aloud the dancing, living threads that twine and make meaning possible. Many was the night when I would sit at the old picnic benches, in the spluttery light from citronella candles, while Mom and Aunt Alice would spin the family tales. About cousins and uncles and aunts I barely knew. About the old country, about County Wexford and the fishing boats that the family owned. About how great-grandpa left the fishing business in his wife's hands and came to the Streets of Gold to seek his fortune. How great-grandma tired of waiting to hear from him, so took ship herself and gave him a helluva surprise one day in New York. About Cousin Alfred in the IRA, who had to flee "the Troubles" as he was a friend of Kevin Barry, the legendary patriot youth who was "hung in the morning." And about how Bridget, or "Bridie," Mom's mom, made a disapproved-of marriage, and how they both were shunned here in the old Irish ghetto in New York until their deaths.

The flip side of Irish lyricism and spirituality is Irish rage, resentment, and shame, the stifled and oppressed part of the people that issued forth in alcoholism and suppressed anger and frustration, the taint of generations. A well-meaning parishioner urged Frank McCourt's masterful *Angela's Ashes* upon me, and I got about thirty pages into the text. When Angela taught her young children the ditty to sing on Fridays while they waited, hungry, hoping that the father had not drunk up his paycheck at the bar,

> *Clap hands, clap hands, 'til Daddy comes home*
> *Daddy has money and Mommy has none*

...I put the book down and never opened it again. Aunt Alice had taught me that same song. That was hitting way too close to home.

But in the spinning and the sacred repetition of the stories, all these people, these events, these places became real for me, part of the landscape of my own life, how I, too, understood myself. They were how my mother understood herself. And the understanding brought both pain and joy.

Years later, when Dad was dead and Mom had been moved out of the house in the throes of Alzheimers, a couple of my brothers began to prepare the old house for sale. They tore up the kitchen linoleum and stared, transfixed. There by the sink, worn into the solid wood of the floor about a half-inch deep, was the unmistakable impression of Mom's two feet, side by side in the place where we had seen her stand day after day, washing by hand yet another load of dishes. The mental image of those prints haunts me now and always will, and fills me with grief and with shame. Lest anyone think that feminism is a '60s relic superseded by a more sophisticated generation, think on those prints. Anyone who really wants to return to a bygone age just doesn't have a very good memory.

Memory and story helped Mom to just get by, day to exhausting day.

We six boys all wove our own fabric of life and success, pain and failure, with the material we had been given. It was during the struggle of

Dad's illness that I think I broke through my adolescent pain and alienation and the heritage of struggle that our parents bequeathed to us all. I broke through, or rather something or someone broke through to me.

One summer I acquired the habit of walking at night and gazing at the stars while hashing and rehashing the Big Issues. One night, as I looked up, the stars seemed to pulse with their own heat and life. And something seemed to pulse with them, there in the night sky, between the stars somehow, in the seeming emptiness, filling the space and somehow filling a space within me as well. I looked and breathed. The night breathed with me. I said aloud, with joy and wonder and reluctance and fear, "OK, if you're really there, then I'll be a priest."

I smile now at that old-world Catholic instinct. If you take God seriously, then dress in black and give up sex.

This Catholic tropism toward priesthood gave me a sense of identity and roots and self-worth at a time when I had little. It gave me a sense of a life waiting for me, a life independent of the old house and my aging parents. It gave me a place and an identity into which I could flee from my pain and my fear and my father's illness and the roil of my adolescence at full boil inside me. It gave me a way out of shyness, as other people in school felt that wanting to be a Catholic priest was baroque and retro and countercultural enough, in 1970s Long Island, to be strangely cool. Ironically, it got me dates, with attractive women who thought I was nice and sensitive and interesting.

The resultant journey took me from a monastic seminary college to a state university where I worked on being very unmonastic. I spent six years in a Catholic religious order, which made it possible for me to spend two years in the southern Philippines as a missionary. My theology was formed in very "liberationist" lines there, amidst an impoverished people who are accustomed to being ground down by oppression and poverty. While there, my physical and emotional health broke down, and I returned Stateside shaken.

Recuperation and healing and reintegration took a number of forms. A kind psychotherapist began to lead me through my inner jungle. I met Diane, or Dina, a young Mexican-American candidate for monastic life herself, and developed a relationship that culminated in our marriage.

My fumbling journey, no roadmap provided, saw me join the Episcopal Church, where I still feel more whole and at home: Catholic but less law-oriented, intrinsically Celtic in some of its worship and culture. I will always be grateful that there was a church that welcomed my questions and showed me hospitality.

I have nothing but gratitude for what I now realize has been a privileged life. I was allowed to have wondrous adventures. I met brave and loving people, men and women of many languages and cultures and places, whose faces and stories are woven into the fabric of whatever good I am and will ever become.

I am now an ordained Episcopal priest, rector of an average-sized church in urban Portland, Oregon, with good-hearted and hardworking folks in its leadership and its pews. We are a good match for one another. To paraphrase Garrison Keillor, Dina and I are still married, and we have three vital, feisty kids who show every promise of becoming splendid adults. We have a ramshackle old house that we scrabble to repair. We are the kind of debt-slaves that you could imagine a clergyman and a teacher with three kids would be. All in all, life is good.

But middle-age is the ancient time for getting lost in "a dark wood," as Dante knew well. At age forty-two, I found restlessness in my soul. I found that I have still my mother's sense of being a permanent alien, my father's unease at how he fits in with the world, this culture, and this economy. I found that the God I have been seeking and trying to serve seems no closer. And I have lived at least half my life, probably more. What do I wish the other half to be? And I bear within me the story of pain and displacement and loneliness that my uprooted Irish and Native Alaskan family bequeathed to me. The stories have etched their patterns on my own soul. They began to lead me on Celtic paths to a holy isle, to grass and carved holy stone and sacred well, and to a rough-hewn town and riverbank that seem to sorrow still with blood and loss.

I fear to only skim the surface of my own life, of the life that is around me. I fear to do no more than skim the surface of God as well.

And the parish? Saints Peter and Paul Episcopal Church is a lovely, vibrant, aging, struggling urban church on a tough street filled with new businesses and car lots, cheek to jowl with prostitution, homelessness, and street crime. This reality was not chosen by the parish founders, who built a small church in a rural town lying outside of Portland. As the urban boundary expanded and the population growth shifted eastward, some in the parish wanted to move and build to follow the growing white suburbs. But the church stayed. A new ethos was acquired in the 1950s, that fat time for "mainline" (now actually "old-line") churches. A young and energetic priest put in place an emphasis on formal worship (chant, incense, heightened symbolism and sense of sacrament, and so on) that Episcopalians call "Anglo-Catholic." In those GI generation days, young families were looking for a church and gravitated especially to the Anglican-style men and boys' choir featured at the parish. Some of the real old-timers still look back on this time as a sort of "golden age," with high attendance and an ambitious building program.

Times change. The choir moved to another church and finally expired in its new setting. The 1960s happened, and people lost that sense of civic Christianity, that "good citizenship" model of church membership, part of the package of being a decent person. Nowadays, perfectly decent people sleep in on Sundays and drive to the coast with their kids. Of course, since the cultural reaction of the 1980s, which gave us a resurgent conservative Protestant "new mainline" in church, culture, and politics, some folks "go to church," but motivations and outcomes have changed profoundly. Here on 82nd Avenue, reasonably progressive mainline Christianity, which takes God and faith and tradition seriously yet is open and honest and welcoming of questions and ambiguity, is a tough sell. Some days it feels like either "no God," law-abiding secularity or marginally criminal secularity in the person of drug-dealing and theft or "rigid God," fundamentalist literalism and individual "me and Jesus" spirituality and right-wing political and cultural agendas. If I personally need a label, it would be something like "progressive postmodern traditional reformed Catholic Celtic Anglican Christian." But then, I weary deeply of labels — they have expiration dates, and today's arguments are tomorrow's jokes. I only put that indigestible mouthful into words to make it clear that I don't feel myself to be a comfortable citizen of anything the surrounding culture produces, religious or not. And as leader of a parish, although I try to keep my personal views clear from folks in order to allow intellectual freedom and conscience, still the longer I am about "priest-craft" the more important I believe authenticity and integrity to be. I'd rather be honest and small and work second jobs than preside over a place that sells a slick and packaged God.

We've had a good time together, the parish and I. I learned to listen to people back in the Philippines, and so I was determined to respect my folks and not have a list of "changes." I buried a lot of the old folks, whom I had grown to love and who had never particularly intimidated me, an advantage of growing up with cranky elderly Irish family. So we learned to trust one another. As a result they let me do a lot together with those folks who knew that change needed to happen in order for the place to stay faithful and viable. New children's and youth programs, an adult faith-formation process based on the baptismal formation of the early Church, a group to help parishioners discern their calls to ministry, more ways to reach out to the broken people on our streets — these and many other attempts helped give us new life.

But still there was a sense in the parish of being at a crossroads — what next, how to speak to a new generation, how to make sense of the raw street where the church has found itself? And in what ways have the parish's older understandings of itself become a problem and not a resource? Parishes, after all, are an old Roman concept of geographical jurisdiction — the name is still used in Louisiana to connote what other states call "counties." If one is within physical range of the parish of St. Nostril's, why then you go to St. Nostril's Church. But the present reality is that people journey to where they feel at home, passing several other churches on the way. And why go to a church at all? According to Mr. Gallup, most Americans have some sort of private faith in God. Why go through the mess and bother of mixing it up with other people, and above all with some religious institution and its baggage and agendas? Better stay with my family, have my private faith, give a little something to charity, maybe read my Bible sometimes if I'm so inspired, or better yet hang Tibetan prayer flags on my porch. Or maybe try one of those new churches that try to meet my every need and make Christianity as culturally palatable and undemanding as possible. What can a dusty little wooden church with an old-fashioned ritual sitting on a rough street have to offer?

Much of what we assume "church" and "faith" and "Christianity" to mean are deeply culturally conditioned notions. Old-line churches like mine are mired in a set of assumptions about commitment, attendance, organization, and the very understanding of church that some today call "Constantinian," a legacy of the establishment of Christianity in the fourth century that bade the followers of Christ drink deeply of the privileges, responsibilities, and social role given them by the ruling Empire. Encourage good citizenship, uphold the Emperor, bless the troops, that sort of thing. Newer churches all too often are just as stuck — becoming the new "mainline" in the modern Empire, helping to elect a president and declaring him "God's anointed," blessing middle American values like individualism, materialism, and entitlement, reducing ethics to privatized sexual behavior (mostly other people's behavior). I hear within myself, within our church, and within many other places a call for a new way, a new way that is old — how to speak truth and honesty and faith and justice and the hunger for God in Christ, the old message that is always new in its hope and always radical and startling. How to get there? Are there any maps, or even clues?

A cartoon once said that one of the most time-honored male rituals is "When things get tough, get out of town." The sacred way to get out of town is called pilgrimage.

I needed a pilgrimage. And I think the parish needed one too. If we couldn't all get on the road, then I figured I'd better get on it and take the parish with me. I realize I had a tall agenda for my journey — the healing of my church, the healing of my own wounds and those of my family. But when the asking is audacious, an audacious God just might be listening.

chapter 3

celtic patterns

A "PATTERN" in the Celtic tradition of pilgrimage is a prescribed set of steps and prayers that one takes on the way to a holy place or says when one arrives. As I look back on how the Celtic Christian "piece" made itself part of my ministry, my life, my soul, the moments along the way look like the seemingly insignificant individual steps and prayers of a pilgrim pattern, long and exhaustive. Only now, looking back, can I see the trail made, missteps, resting places, and all.

It was the stories that shaped and molded me from the first.

Family stories I was told, and like a little stone I was shaped slowly by the drops that fell until I was carved with furrows, or perhaps Celtic spirals.

In amidst the tales of colorfully dysfunctional relations were tales of priests and penitents, saints and scoundrels. I began to get a shadowy sense of a spiritual world peopled by angels and sprites and ghosts as well, where blessing and even luck was to be had by the knowledgable or the devout or the merely fortunate. I heard the name of Patrick, of course, and was shown party-line images of him dressed demurely like a Roman bishop in spotless mitre and chasuble. He was either holding an outsized shamrock as if he'd grown it himself or was bending over a squiggly snake or two, looking disappointed in something the snake had said or done. And I heard the name Brigid for the first time, breathed with the deepest reverence by my mother. No doubt she put her soul's longing and grief for her own mother Brigid into the sigh, but still the name was redolent of power and grace. She knew nothing of the real Brigid, other than assuring me that she was a saint. Again, the picture in the party-line pious booklet for Catholic children was a disappointment — Brigid was painted as a Roman-looking medieval nun with a look of faint gastric upset masked with a slight smile on her rosy face.

But something spoke, something deep — something older, something mysterious, something a bit wild and even dangerous. Ringed stone crosses, beehive-shaped huts, tales of Vikings axing monks apart for their gold. But no further information was forthcoming at that time.

It was years later, when I was a student in a Spanish-founded Catholic missionary order, that the hunger was rekindled.

I was a novice for the Claretian Missionaries in the Philippines, two harrowing yet glorious years. The modest bookshelves in the dusty cinderblock novitiate house contained a book on the spirituality of "the desert" — referring to the third to the sixth century or so and the great romanticized flight to the African and Middle Eastern deserts by fervent Christians. They fled from what they saw as the spiritual shipwreck of Christianity as it became the "established faith" of the late Roman Empire, and sought a way to be simple and clear about following Christ and seeking God. Living alone or in small informal groups around a spiritual father or mother (*abba* or *amma*), they were the first "monks" (Greek *monachos:* those alone, presumably with God). Their lives and even more their "sayings," Zen-like in their clarity and parable-like in their simplicity, became the inspiration for century upon century of passionate folks who hungered for immediate experience of God and stripped life and faith down to their essentials.

It was the wild desert that gave the early Celtic Church its heart and soul.

The desert came to the Celtic lands at the fringe of the Empire by way of old Gaul, modern France. John Cassian brought the desert style of monasticism there, and Celtic seekers as well as missioners bound for the Celtic lands drank there of its spirit. So the kind of Christianity that grew up in ancient Ireland and Scotland and Brittany in France, in Wales and Cornwall and the Isle of Man, in Northumbria in England, was a Christianity which honored the passionate seeker and the pilgrim, with a taste for the desert and a gut-level sense that since God was not tame then the people of God had no need of being tame either. The church in Ireland in particular was a monastic church, with abbots and abbesses in the lead and the clan enclosures, the *tuath*, becoming the monastic communities with people of many states of life within. Honoring pilgrims and pilgrimage, seeking and serving God with warrior passion, seeing that God in the awesome beauty and power of creation as well as in all things beautiful and creative, being culturally more open to women in positions of leadership, this church flourished while the Empire died and the form of church allied with the Empire either faltered or slowly became the new Empire. Eventually the two ways, the Celtic way and the reconstituted Roman way, met and began to clash and to mix. But today the "alternative narrative" of the Celtic way of faith is being re-read and re-told, re-imagined and re-tried, as yet another form of the Empire withers and declines all around us. As we seek an authentic way of faith that is vital and communal, flexible yet passionate, that reaches out to the broken and makes whole our own lives, that loves the world and does not spend energy in condemning those who do not fit by way of race or gender or sexual orientation or language or culture or by any other rigid standard, I think it is time to seek and bring forth something new by unearthing something old.

chapter 4

tragic town

W HEN I COULD NOT wade through *Angela's Ashes* for the pain it
evoked, I realized how deeply the tales of misery and struggle
had graven themselves upon my soul. Dreadful is the memory. More
dreadful still is the forgetting, so that the wound on the soul gapes and
stinks and continues its legacy of rage and parsimony and depression
and shame. For the Irish are by nature a generous people, as are all
the Celtic folk. On Iona I made a casual remark to a fellow pilgrim, an
American Franciscan priest, about "Irish guilt." He replied that in his
opinion it was not so much a matter of Irish guilt as it was Irish shame:
hospitality was renowned and sacred among the Irish, but the misery and
legacy of famine and poverty meant that there was not enough to feed
your own and also share so much as a morsel with a stranger. Perhaps the
proverbial Irish-Catholic guilt and Irish alcoholic self-medication all have
their roots in this dispossession. Starving on your own land. Starving
and cuffed around wherever the "wild geese" of exiles and émigrés flew,
whether to America or Australia or wherever a door grudgingly opened.
Starved and cuffed, until you got confident and numerous and influential
enough to start cuffing back.

Beyond New Age Celtic romanticism and Irish sentimentality, the
Irish-American dewy-eyed wish to find the little village where one's family hailed from and, just like John Wayne in *The Quiet Man*, have all the
men in the pub buy you a round and say, "The men of Innisfree bid you
welcome home," are some harsh truths. Poverty. Hopelessness. Bigotry.
Legacies of violence and fratricidal war.

I've been very privileged in my lifetime, so I need to be very humble
and reticent about claiming this pain as my own. But the stories were

told, and since they were told, in a very real way it is my own. Growing up, I had no doubt of it.

My mother and Alice's canon of stories told the tale in this fuller way: in a small town in County Wexford, on the southeastern end of Ireland, Mom and Alice's family, the Morrisseys, lived. They were fishing people, and had a small fleet of boats. They kept the boats at a place called "Morrissey's Bank." Mom's mother was named Bridget, called "Bridie" by her family, and, judging from the one old daguerrotype that has survived, was every inch the Irish beauty — wide-set eyes, heart-shaped face, lovely form visible even beneath the fabric folds and the bustle.

Bridie, by all accounts, was the darling of her parents' eyes and had her share of swains. But the one on which her eye and heart alighted was not, by her parents' thinking, the proper one. He was one Patrick Flood, a penniless young man from Kilkenny. He was described as red-haired and a bit dreamy. Dark-haired young Bridie fell deeply in love with him. So deeply, in fact, that her mother's ire and her family's rejection and shunning meant little. They all emigrated at about the same time — first Grandpa Morrissey to seek his fortune on the gold-paved streets of New York, then some months later, not telling him she was doing so, his wife, who sold the fishing boats and ran into him on a New York street. Surprise! "Honey, I've sold the fleet!" Apparently the whole clan, more or less, came over and through Ellis Island at roughly the same time, including Bridie and Patrick. Although they lived within a couple of blocks of the rest of the clan on New York's Upper West Side, the familial excommunication was still in effect, and the relations would cross the street rather than speak to them.

A girl was born to Bridie and Patrick there: Margaret, my mother. A boy too: Thomas. Patrick found work "pulling beers" in a basement bar.

It was not long before tuberculosis, one of the epidemics raging in those old ghettos, killed Patrick. The sawdust on the bar's floor and the bad air of old New York no doubt contributed to the swiftness of his death. Apparently, after his death, the family ban persisted, and Bridie, alone in a strange, pre–New Deal country with no resources and no emotional support, just gave up. The family canon spoke of it as "a broken heart"; perhaps today a diagnosis of clinical depression would be rendered. At any rate, she would take a penny or so and buy a bag of cookies and just sit on a bench by the river, near the present site of the United Nations building, and she and little Margaret would eat the cookies and watch the river. Perhaps, gazing into the increasingly polluted waters, she was reminded of the dark and dirty flow through New Ross, her Irish home town. I believe this fragment of experience provided my mother's sole memory of her own mother: she recalled a cold, windy, bright day; water flowing, and herself standing in a short red coat. She remembers the face of a very pretty, very sweet and sad-looking woman gazing down at her. She remembers an infant asleep in a carriage: my uncle.

Within six months the cholera took Bridie and infant Uncle Thomas too.

Then and only then, so the oral chronicle says, did the remaining Morrisseys sail in to "rescue" little Peg. But the first one in the door of the apartment was the mother, who, before she did anything else, burned every photograph of Patrick in the iron stove.

In later years Mom never lost her bitterness over her father being so taken from her. And in the Zen-like directness of speech of her later years, she would agonize to me about seeing her parents again. "I'm looking forward to seeing them after I die. But they were so young when they died. I'm an old lady. Will they recognize me?"

Even though she was taken in by cousins who loved her and whom she called Mom and Pop, she never lost that sense of being outside, of being a stranger, of not belonging, of having lost who she really was and how she could be really secure and safe and known.

I've told the story many times over the years. At first I told it idly, as a child will chime in when family stories are offered. Then I told it as an entertaining tale, interesting in its sadness and long-ago loss. Today I find it harder and harder to tell, hard to write — it sings darkly of a sorrow that I fear. Perhaps telling the story so many times, in so many places, has made it my own, has spoken that sorrow in the emptiness of my own heart. Perhaps since I am old enough to have known loss and defeat and aloneness and have felt many a hand grow cold in death while holding my own, I can hear the story now with all its echoes.

It has notes of triumph and hope as well. Peg survived, grew, married, raised a family, found something of home with the man whose people and personal life also knew exile and loss. She named her fourth boy Keith Thomas, after the infant lost and buried in a poor New York grave. And we have named my red-haired, graceful first daughter Bridget. How Mom and, I think, Grandma would have loved her. And perhaps, in the Celtic and folk-Catholic way of viewing things, they do so now. I like to believe so.

Chapter 5

In the Connection

EVERY CHRISTIAN needs a rabbi, or, at least, every clergyperson does, to keep us honest and to show us what real scholarship is all about. The Holy One, blessed be he, has loaned me a rabbi or two from time to time.

One of these, Lisa Goldstein, last heard from wowing them at a Hillel ministry on the West Coast, I knew in St. Louis, when we mixed up my confirmation class and her bar/bat Mitzvah class for some conversation on chosen questions. Most intellectually stimulating two hours I ever spent doing youth ministry.

I once asked Rabbi Lisa, "What is the Holy?" Pondering a rabbinic moment, she answered, "Connection. People to God, God to earth, people to earth, person to person. Connection." I've never improved on that.

Connection broken has been a constant in my life.

Some of this I have inherited. Being the child of two people who were deeply wounded, displaced, and the children themselves of broken and disconnected people has handed me a script for disconnection.

Some of this was given to me by time and place. The Long Island of the '70s was a tumultuous place in which to be a teenager: fading ghosts of '60s activism, disillusionment, collapsing economy, lots of alcohol and drugs available and seemingly "everyone" doing it, lots of sex available in a pre-HIV-conscious atmosphere. My father died when I was sixteen, my Mom was aged and struggling to know herself after years of being defined as "Mom" and "wife." My brothers, each one of us as basically individualistic as the next, were all much older and far more like uncles than anything else. Each had his family, his life.

Much of this rootlessness I chose: to move to Chicago, to accept the chance to be immersed in Southeast Asia for two years, to move to a different church and a different coast, to put lots of geography between myself and the weight of history and family and my own role.

My tropism toward Catholicism and the Catholic image of God, toward priesthood and toward monastic life, was both an expression of, and an attempt to find a way out of, disconnection and alienation and personal pain and unresolved self-image and maturity and sexuality, health and pathology and refuge all at once. Not surprisingly, neither monasticism nor the Roman Catholic Church spoon-fed me any answers.

But they did provide me with much that has endured. Catholicism gave me a sense of roots in an older culture and worldview, one that has changed and been deconstructed but still had endured. Providing a language for addressing the Holy, for addressing Mystery, awakened in me a hunger to do so always, and so Catholic Christianity remains the language of my soul on a deep level, although I have also listened to and learned of the soul-language of others. Priesthood gave me a sense that my own roil of impulses and contradictions might actually do someone else some good, that I could speak to the journey and the struggle and the pain of others.

Monasticism gave me something else. As I sought community, the ideal of a common project of life, a common vision, and living it out day to day together with others spoke to me deeply. Monastic prayer, based on regular recitation of the Psalms, appealed ever since I discovered the Psalms at an early age and was thrilled by their raw, direct speech, peeling away artifice and seeking nothing less than direct converse between real people and a living God. And the tension between "inner" and "outer," lofty goal and nitty-gritty day-to-day living, the shattering immediacy of an immanent God and the sardonic realism of "We're in this for the long haul" appealed to me deeply. As did the romanticism, the anachronistic appeal of medieval imagery, cloister and cowl and chant, the implied critique and rejection of all that our culture has become which, I blithely assumed, was basically bad.

Many years later, I come to myself and realize that though I don't live in a cloister, I don't wear a robe with cowl and cincture, I have found my monasticism. My chapel is my parish church. My cell is my body, or my bedroom as I rub sleep from my eyes and struggle to focus on Psalms and readings before helping with feeding and launching the kids. My cloister is the world and my life, lived quite strictly between home and church, my two communities. My poverty is dependence on God and simplicity and debt-slavery mandated by raising three kids and helping to feed five people. My forgetting of myself is made real in my relationship with my wife, learning to love and to be loved and to make love and to forgive and to fight for dear life on a daily basis. Monastic indeed. The cloister would be a vacation by contrast, at least until I caught up on sleep and quiet.

But I wouldn't take the cloister back. Here is where I have learned and am learning to be human. Marriage and family life and the path of my existence has been graced, has been my salvation.

But no way of life, no one place, no career, no lover, has contained the basic answers posed by the questions of my own soul. They have paved the road, formed the signposts and the inns where I have been refreshed. They have given me hope and life.

The face of God remains obscure, perhaps because the masks change and are changing. And I still seek essential connection, with God and with the earth and with past and with present and with pain and with those around me and with myself.

That's how this journey began: knowing that my basic search, the mystery for which I have been born and placed here, has not yet ended. Perhaps it is enough to say with honesty that it has only truly begun.

chapter 6

setting out,
seeking the blessing

PHIL COUSINEAU, in his exquisite book *The Art of Pilgrimage*, speaks eloquently of the profound restlessness and sense of absence, of emptiness, that presages the decision to go on pilgrimage. Life and vitality itself feel absent, and the usual means to re-engage life and vitality do not work. Even if the notion seems strange, one begins to hope for a rediscovery of vitality on the road.

Such was my own case. Every fiber in my being ached with a kind of weariness, perhaps a gentle depression, but one which I felt sure would be resistant to any round of talk therapy. This ache had far more to do with loss and longing and seeking. But seeking what?

The years since my journey sideways, as it were, into the Episcopal Church from Rome, the busy years which began when we arrived penniless but almost debt-free with a six-week-old infant at Seabury-Western Seminary, have been kind all in all. I spent a busy four years doing youth work and the assistant-priest thing at Emmanuel, a happy but exhaustingly busy suburban parish outside of St. Louis. I moved from there to Portland, and a real ecclesiastical contrast — Saints Peter and Paul, smaller, money-challenged, urban, working-class, with lovely generous people who have worked hard to maintain the small gray A-frame ark that lies along a main commercial strip. Deficit budgets, minimal administrative help, recent bitter controversies about sexuality and whether one should address the Deity in the second person as "you" or "thou," lots of funerals among a strong strata of World War II–generation folks whom I have come to love. It has been a good place to live and to work, a good place to raise the children (the third one rode west in our used minivan "in utero" and so missed the sun on mesas and tumbleweeds on the highway). My beloved wife came to treasure Portland and only wished she could pick it up and move it to within three hours of Chicago and her very traditional, very close Mexican-American family.

It has been eleven years but has not even felt like eleven weeks. I want to talk to whoever keeps pressing the "fast forward" button as I get older.

Parishioners and colleagues noticed me seeming frazzled, with a kind of tiredness that a night's sleep couldn't cure. The verve, the passion for justice and for meaning and for truth and for God had faded and was not to be renewed by a church service or a meeting with my spiritual director or a weekend off or a day at some monastery.

Meanwhile change and ferment were in the air. The angst and hand-wringing of the "mainline" churches, while the culture seems to either forget the "Christian thing" or turn to highly conservative presentations of the Gospel, has dominated the church landscape throughout my ministry. But in endless reflection and conversation I found more and more people who just wanted to be authentic, to follow Christ and live in community and reach out to the broken and to seek reconciliation.

And Celtic things were in the air. Bob Ladehoff, our bishop at the time, had all us clergy read the fanciful little book *Celtic Gifts* by Robert Van Der Weyer. A fictional English bishop works an "extreme makeover" of his diocese across Celtic lines, by thinking out of established patterns, being open to new directions, and welcoming the many gifts of the people of the community. When asked why he chose the book, Bob said enigmatically, "I thought it was interesting."

Meanwhile I talked of being worn out. I invoked the agreement we had signed, which requires a sabbatical every five years. The parish did nothing but encourage me.

I thought briefly of using the time to go to school and take some gee-whiz courses on how to make my parish (a) much bigger, (b) much more modern, (c) much more wealthy, but the idea made me feel so sick I almost retched.

I thought of pursuing courses and events all around the country relating to storytelling. I love story and see myself in fantasy as a professional storyteller, so this had some allure. But this still didn't quite seem the vehicle. I saw in mind's eye a succession of one-and-a-half star motels and endless corn dogs washed down in the hot sun with Country Time lemonade. I did not thrill at the notion.

I still don't remember who said, "Why don't you go to Ireland?"

It might have been a clergy friend. It might have been my long-suffering wife. I *do* know that she shocked me exceedingly, she who takes me on when I say "yes" to too much church stuff, when she suddenly said, "I think that if you have the chance to go to Ireland, you should just go."

I don't see myself as the kind of person who gets to go to places like Europe. I see myself as the kind of person who gets to go to the beach for a day since he's a lucky-to-live-in-Portland kind of person. I'm the guy who looks forward to vacation so he doesn't have to set the clock and so he can read for at least half the day before taking the kids to the public pool or starting to paint the gutters.

Even thinking of going to Ireland, ditching the family and going, was the most incredible stretch of the imagination.

But it began to come together. Parishioners especially seemed to think it natural that I would want to go to the land of both my spiritual and my familial roots.

One parishioner e-mailed me and told me to dream and to go, that it was important not only for me but for our parish, which like me also hesitates to dream big. "Besides," she added, "Brigid and Columba tell me that they want you home for a week."

I cried as I read this and still get tears in my eyes. I had not realized that I longed so for home, and that I longed for the call home to come from ancient lips, the saints of my people.

My spiritual guide, a wise old priest that every son of an Episcopalian for miles around consults at one time or another, told me to ask, ask for the money, ask the bishop, ask the parish, and ask again. It's hard for me to ask for things. But I did.

I learned of a seminar which was, to me, the final door opening. I had for some time received e-mailings from a group called "Storyfest Ministries," an organization founded and run by Bob and Kelly Wilhelm, lifelong students of the power of story and myth. They were recruiting folks for a seminar on sacred story offered on Iona, the ancient holy isle off the west coast of Scotland, fabled monastic settlement of great St. Columba. It couldn't be better.

The parish coughed up an amazing amount of money for us, well over two thousand dollars. My experience years ago planning summer mission trips for teenagers served me well as I mapped out a budget for five weeks. I wrote this up, including the seminar fee, and sent it off to my bishop. He promptly remitted the balance.

It was with shock that I realized I was going.

Something in me didn't feel worth the support and the gifts of people to make the journey possible. But I learned of the uncanny power and fact of doors opening, of people affirming and agreeing that it was important that I take this journey. I had been given a pilgrim's blessing without even a sprinkle of holy water or a whiff of incense.

I gazed at Internet images of Iona with wonder. They might have been images of the moon, and I an astronaut filled with anticipation and not a little fear.

From my two years spent in the Catholic missions of Southeast Asia, I carry a few inner souvenirs. One is a romanticism of utter freedom, remembering the times I hopped buses into the back country carrying only an over-the-shoulder bag, equipped only with a sparse knowledge of one dialect and faith mixed with naiveté. I still long for those days, and have this impossible image of myself still capable, on some level, of breaking free and taking off. I think I'm possessed of a strange mix of the genuine spirit of pilgrimage, the intoxication of the *peregrinatio Cristi*, the "pilgrimage of Christ" of the wandering Celtic Christians, mixed with an adolescent desire to just cut loose and wander off at a moment's notice.

Another, less attractive, souvenir of that time in Asia is a lingering anxiety about long periods of solitude. My cultural alienation and personal isolation, the only American together with a Spanish priest and Filipino students, bubbled and brewed with my inner spiritual and emotional turmoil to cause a profound psychic and spiritual crisis. I fought panic attacks in the last months of my time in Asia, and only ameliorated them with time and talk therapy back Stateside. Still, on retreats, or during protracted solitary periods, I find myself not experiencing those attacks but remembering the fear and sometimes feeling anxious about their possible return.

This pilgrimage would not be just beer and giggles. It would be a chance to wrestle some very personal demons. After all, it is not God alone who lives in the desert. There are beasts and bandits, danger and dread. The worst ones are the ones within.

I also feared disappointment. I remember visiting my brother Rick in Virginia when I was a teenager. I had never been out of New York before this, and I distinctly remember marveling that earth still looked like earth, grass was green, trees were still wooden and tall in such a foreign and exotic setting like another state. I worried that Ireland and even Iona would turn out to be utterly ordinary, and that I would return weary of the earth and of the same dirt that covers its whole surface.

In and amidst all these conflicting feelings, lots had to be done.

Cousineau's book on pilgrimage became very important to me. It was a frame of reference in which I learned that naming each step on the journey was sacred, each moment of preparation was important. As I prepared, I realized with a shiver of anticipation and apprehension that the journey had already begun.

The parish was surprisingly easy to leave for a while. Over Thai noodle soup, Lindsay Warren, a wise retired priest who would be bemused by the first adjective, agreed to take over the parish during my month away. The wardens and vestry, the lay officers, were unremitting in their support. The whole place seemed of one voice that this trip was a good idea, that I needed and deserved it. Perhaps they needed to be cut off from me for a while too. The newsletter editor asked me to submit an e-mail partway through my time. I agreed to try, but privately was not confident of my desire to do so. I love the parish but felt worn down by its demands. I needed to completely "check out" for a bit.

Public ministry is a wondrous yet arduous way to live and to make some sort of living. In a postmodern, "post-Christian" era the life contains very specific stresses. Respect for the clergy as a whole is decreased, while expectations rise. The clergy person is the last great generalist who is expected to be theologian, teacher, worship leader, spiritual guide, counselor, yet be literate in fundraising, physical plant management, long-range development, architecture, grounds keeping, conflict resolution, and a host of other tasks that parishioners tend to assume "someone will take care of." In the size of parish that is mine, there is a small handful of paid staff compensated on an extremely part-time basis, so I alone am the highly visible, full-time paid staff person — in fact, my compensation is nearly half the budget. In the older model, the priest is the resident nice guy, around to give comfort and to smooth feathers and to keep the more fractious people from rending one another, to pick up the trash and set up for the weddings, to call the exterminator when the ants appear in the kitchen. If I'm not careful, my week is spent in this kind of management.

Like many another professions I am sure, "They didn't teach us that in school."

Do you know what it is when a cloud of gnats, an endless array of minor clutter, rises each day from the earth and surrounds your desk, surrounds your life? I suspect you do.

It's not "burn-out." It's "disillusion-out." Is this what I wish the rest of my life and energy to be?

I don't know what I expected to find on pilgrimage — some insight? Courage to take the next step, to change my life? Or strength to recommit to the same task?

In the meanwhile, between Lindsay, the deacon, and the lay leadership, the parish was going to be in good hands.

Home was much harder to leave. It came as a sort of surprise to realize we really are a close-knit family. We're not apart very often. Dina was as good as her word and worked hard to put a brave face on things. She made a paper chain and a calendar for the children to mark off the days that I would be gone; also she posted a map with the air routes highlighted to London, Glasgow, Dublin. We worked out how and how often I would call.

I worked feverishly around the house, doing lots of odd small things to ready it for late fall. They all felt like Last Things. There was an odd note of finality about it. I thought often of medieval pilgrims and how it was common for them to die while on pilgrimage for a whole host of reasons — the old pilgrim trails to Santiago de Compostela, to Rome, and to Jerusalem are dotted to this day with pilgrim graves, pilgrim cemeteries. It may sound melodramatic and foolish to those who hop international flights regularly and with ease. But I think the air of solemnity was important. Pilgrimage by nature needs to have a note of finality to it. If one is truly going into the presence of the Holy, one really doesn't know what to expect. The presence of the Holy can be disastrous. And when one is a pilgrim, one is seeking death and re-birth. It seems silly to expect this to be easy or risk free.

I made several treks to a AAA travel agent, a nice, tender-tough lady who just barely forbore from calling me "hon." We spoke matter-of-factly about Scottish trains and ferries, Glasgow hotels, Irish rental cars. It all sounded so exotic.

Feeling very responsible, I paid for traveler's insurance and read the amount on the slip of paper. Like George Bailey in *It's a Wonderful Life,* I felt worth more dead than alive. If the plane went down, between that and the church insurance, Dina and the kids would have debts paid, house mortgage paid, be able to live for about a year. After that, it would be up to them. Not bad. I hate our debts so much that for a fleeting second the image of my death gave me a sense of grim satisfaction: cashed out at last.

At Goodwill I got a small piece of luggage with a retractable handle for pulling. I liked it but later decided it must have been meant for a child, for the handle was so short that it caused backache over long distances. On the top was a neat slit covered with a strip of green duct tape, the Universal Adhesive that holds our world together. I speculated that the cut had come from a drug search, giving the little case an aura of danger. I also got a thin blue pullover windbreaker from Goodwill, which worked great on dry days but clung like soggy paper in a rain.

It rains a lot in Ireland.

I bought a pair of hiking shoes that turned out to be too small for me. Hence the shoes became penance devices, making my feet pay for all my past sins each step of the way. In all honesty, a few weeks in tight shoes is not a bad trade for my track record. But I thought often of the penitents of old putting stones in their shoes.

I learned a lot for next time. Long handles, Scotch-guard, and size ten *wide,* well-broken in.

I thought enviously of the old images I'd seen of medieval pilgrims to Santiago — wide-brimmed hats, cloaks, small leather pouches slung over the shoulder, staves with drinking gourds suspended, nothing more. Sounds good to me, I thought, as I surveyed my swollen backpack and green duct-taped case. Dina for her part marveled at how little I packed. In my desire to travel unencumbered is my longing for freedom, and even for escape. Which is my true self? My life encumbered by commitments, relationships, dependencies, people, debts, and obligations, or myself walking alone with nothing but some faltering faith and a small bag? Or are both true, both authentic, both part of the same pilgrimage?

chapter 7

voyage

IN THE DAYS leading up to my leaving, I became deeply aware of something frazzled deep down in my being, something frayed and dry like the rope ends my father kept in our basement. Like those rope ends, I sensed how rough the loose ends of my inner being were, how threadbare and how doubtful the strength. I was more and more excited about leaving. But I was filled with foreboding as well. Would I come back? Would I *want* to come back? When I returned, would I want to return to the life and the profession I knew? Would I lose my mind from the solitude over there? Would I find God and ancient saints and ancient faith, or simply old stones, mossy and dead?

I packed my scant things in my ominously slashed *French Connection* case and the brown backpack. A thick sweater and one of my old tweed coats would have to do for protection against the weather — that and an English black wool cap that was a bequest from a parishioner's priest father. It fit snugly and shed water like a slightly odorous duck.

Over the years, I have developed the habit of daily reciting the Office, a traditional structure of psalms, readings, and prayers. When I travel, I fret a little about which version of the Office to bring — how light the books, what readings they cover, and so on. A parish family gave me as a surprise gift a copy of a graceful book, *Celtic Prayers from Iona* by J. Philip Newell. The prayers are lyrical, based on the earthy rhythm of the folk-prayers of the Scottish Hebrides, which Alexander Carmichael patiently recorded and transcribed in the nineteenth century. The lovely calligraphy soothed me, the Celtic poetry invited me to prepare my soul for bleak green fields and rushing gray waters. With this slender book I brought a tiny leather-bound Bible, which I could barely read then and not at all now. It was the tiny size that captivated me — it looked like a pilgrim's book.

I brought a flashlight, which I almost never used but worked well as a metaphor for the need for light in dark places. A slender folding traveling clock which turned out to be invaluable — most B&B rooms did not have their own clocks or at least did not have clocks that worked. On nights when I felt desolate, the tiny gray rectangle of the clock with its geometric numbers switching regularly spoke of a sense of order that was oddly comforting.

I brought a Roman Catholic–style rosary, one that my father-in-law had rescued from a washing machine in the laundromat he managed. I have often carried prayer beads of various configurations, but I had a clear feeling that I wanted to import nothing foreign to Ireland, save perhaps myself. Although the Marian emphasis in Irish Catholicism gradually supplanted the older indigenous cult of the local saints, still it is strong and present and I felt that it was somehow fitting that I bring Our Lady's rosary.

I brought a stack of papers having to do with many things — car rental, hotel reservations, the storytelling seminar on Iona. I packed a small journal and a couple of good pens. I brought some American postcards for symbolic gifts — another piece of advice from Mr. Cousineau, who counsels being generous with the land and people whom you meet. I brought the latest edition of the "Let's Go" guidebook to Ireland, and what felt like a brick of traveler's checks, about which I worried neurotically — I feared getting robbed and being stranded somewhere. The "Let's Go" book advised a money belt, and I often regretted not getting one.

So, dear pilgrim, I do advise these things: get the money belt, buy yourself a good waterproof coat, break in your shoes thoroughly and make sure they're loose. Consider pants other than jeans — I love denim, but it's hot in summer and not too warm in winter, and is heavy and deathly when wet. Be sparing with the books you bring. In retrospect I wish I had taken notes from the "Let's Go" book instead of lugging the whole thing along.

When one goes on pilgrimage, one discovers the extra burdens one lugs through life itself — stuff, agendas, wounds, fears. The road (or the airports, or the buses, or the ferries) quickly educates one as to what one has carried, what one could have and should have left behind. And what one can learn to leave behind when one returns.

Murphy's Law said I'd get sick on the eve of departure, like the last time I had left town for any length of time. But I was as healthy as a horse when we got up before sunrise and piled sleepy children into the dented family minivan for the run to the airport.

Saying goodbye was a kind of a death.

My wife Dina and I have a fiery but nearly always supportive relationship. We both have wounds that understand one another. We're both at heart somewhat conservative people, raised in conservative religions and cultures, who nevertheless were deeply shaped by the iconoclasm of the '60s and '70s when we came of age. We fight hard but make up just as passionately, which makes the fights forgettable. When we hugged and kissed, then pulled apart, the feeling was physically painful, like the ripping of flesh. She cried. I just got disoriented, my hands fidgeting with nothing.

Looking at the kids standing with tears in their eyes I awoke to just how fiercely precious they are to me and what an enormous thing must be driving my soul that would take me far from them, far from whatever protection and comfort I could offer. I had a sudden, insane image of a stranger breaking into the house by night and the children sobbing "Daddy" while they were being hurt. I almost didn't go. I'm not sure at that moment what put me on the plane. Wooden-legged, I limped stiffly aboard and sat, feeling relieved and grieved and foolish all at once. I was doing something utterly mad and impractical, something utterly out of character in my very structured little life. I told myself, sitting in the coarse airline seat with the none-too-fresh airplane air blowing over me from the inevitable overhead asexual nipple, that people do this all the time. People leave their spouses and families for days, weeks, months for a whole host of reasons. I should just get over it. But it was no good. I could not get over it. I never did, and I never will.

In my journal, I wrote:

I leave my heart behind,
Sweet children and warm sweet wife
Who scorches me,
Then heals and saves.
Sweet eyes tore and
Clutched at my skin —
My eyes tried to
Remember them forever.

I don't fly well. It has to be a damn good reason indeed to get me into what I think of as a beer can with wings. I don't white-knuckle, but I sweaty-palm, especially during takeoffs. I tried not to leave wet stains on the armrest as I thought, "If it goes down, the mortgage is paid." That is a morbid kind of debt-consolidation.

I don't remember much of the domestic flight. It must have happened. I usually don't chat up fellow passengers, so I stayed lost in my thoughts. I think there were movies, clearly not memorable. I prayed using the Iona book. I thought, I fidgeted. As the plane barreled along, I thought of the Wild Geese, the ancient Wild Hunt of the Celts and the Saxons, the flight that the modern Irish and Scots used to name their own departure from their lands to escape poverty and the law. I thought of how coddled a life I had lived, not like them, not like Patrick and Bridie and all. They creaked across the Atlantic in steerage, never to see their own land again, just hoping to find work and a place to stay. Here I jetted with suitcase crammed with traveler's checks, credit cards snug in the wallet, maps and books and reservation sheets telling me exactly where to go, when, for how long, when to return. I thought of all those true Wild Geese, the lone exiles who fled and died, so many, who built communities and nations so that their sentimental descendants could buy coach seats and fly back to where they left. I imagined them laughing and telling me exactly where to go with my worries, and not with a computer printout, either. I smiled silently at then while accepting their laughter.

The travel-weary flight attendant announced that "passengers bound for London" (me! I thought in amazement) would "experience an equipment change in Washington" (sounded like we would each be personally rewired) and "board the 'over-water plane.'" In my journal I tried to sketch my concept of an "over-water plane" — it looked vaguely pregnant, and large-bodied enough to float if need be. That last detail was more hopeful on my part than anything else. At least the Titanic had a few lifeboats. . . .

Brendan and his monks, during their voyage to the Land of the Blessed, which may have been North America, celebrated Mass on a round island which turned out to be the back of a whale. I could scarcely find a stranger or more perilous vessel than that.

The "over-water plane" turned out to be a very businesslike-looking machine, large, squat, and powerful-looking with massive engines. It looked like it believed itself capable of crossing the ocean. I chose to believe what it believed.

The interior was pleasantly roomy. Even in coach we were each equipped with a television screen, the technological age's talisman of assurance. Clearly being over-water had its advantages. I wish now that I'd been priest enough to wonder if there was a baptismal message there, that being "over water" meant a larger life or some such. But at the time I sat, still numb from the goodbye to my family, still getting over being a "passenger bound for London," wishing the airline powers that be would turn on the TVs while on the ground so that I could fidget in peace.

The plane began to slowly fill up with passengers, a far more cosmopolitan lot than those with whom I had crossed the U.S. Languages, lovely to hear — German, French, Spanish, some lovely minor keys that I assumed were Arabic. Clothes became more stylish, or exuberantly less so, or just more exotic by Pacific Northwest standards. The seat next to me was taken by an ample elderly lady, draped with much colored cloth and various jangling gold doodads, who mumbled throughout takeoff and the first part of the flight.

Which the plane managed quite well, I must say. The jet shouldered its way into the air and purred powerfully into the east. I was content at last to let the jet, and of course its crew, pursue its business and find London without me trying to steer it by leaning side to side in the seat. I found something else to do.

I read prayers and Scripture again, from my two small books. I quickly gave up on the novel I had brought, A Monk Swimming by Malachy McCourt, brother of Frank — journal of an immigrant Irishman covering up his pain and aloneness by wisecracking and drinking, cracking heads and swan-diving into as many different beds as he could. I have nothing particularly against wisecracking and drinking, having done a fair share of both. The head-cracking and swan-diving are both a bit destructive in different measures and in different ways, but still quite human. But Malachy, a good writer to be sure as must run in Clan McCourt, just wasn't where I was for this trip. He became excess baggage, and I finally left him in a B&B in New Ross. Sometimes it is hard to predict what will emerge as excess baggage.

I channel-surfed and fidgeted with the TV screen. Again, I cannot remember a single film. What's the last memorable film you saw on an airplane?

But as the miles fell behind the plane something did change. Resignation and surrender to the journey became something else: freedom. I was a pilgrim, alone, but free save for what I bore in my two packs. I had settled my affairs as best I could. My wife was competent and my kids, although young, had their own schools and lives and helped around the house. If I died, they would be cared for. It was time to be present to this journey, to be here, now, alive. To seek, and to be attentive, lest what I sought present itself to me and I be so self-absorbed that I would miss it.

The ample lady next to me began a determined but unsuccessful fight with her TV screen and volume control, in the process increasing her own mumble-volume. I finally identified the mumbles as Spanish. It was like a touch of home. I leaned over a bit (just a hair; today's airline seats are so close that leaning over at all nearly constitutes sexual assault) and asked her in Spanish if she needed help.

She looked startled and slightly suspicious, then peered hopefully out from beneath heavy-lidded eyes. "You speak Spanish?"

"A little. You have no sound?"

"Yes, it is broken."

"With your permission." With the dreadful technical competence that the younger can demonstrate over the elder, I leaned over and punched the volume button until even I could hear her headphones blaring.

She smiled slightly then and accepted my further technical consultation with the air of one accustomed to being helped. As for me, I've always had elderly aunts or a mom around to help, so I felt right at home — her gift to me. Still in something of a mumble, she told me that she was traveling to London to meet some family member, then on to Spain and finally to the Canary Islands. I rolled "Islas Canarias" around silently on my tongue, pleased at the taste, wishing I had some Canary wine with which to wash it down.

In speaking with her, I adopted a friendly passive reticence that I would maintain throughout my journey — I was asked little about myself, so I offered little. She was the first of many to never hear that I was a priest or that my journey was a pilgrimage.

Many air conversations just end, with the unspoken etiquette that although one's face remains inches from one's companion's it is nevertheless time to be silent and allow each to withdraw into some inner solitude. Our conversation did not last long, and the lady listened contentedly to her headset, mumble-free at last.

There is a timelessness to long air flight, or rather a vacuum of time. Light came and went, people slept or awoke. As I did not carry a watch, I had long lost any sense of what time my body assumed it to be, or what time on earth it was where the plane was positioned.

A change came over the compartment. People began slowly, almost imperceptibly, to stir and move about a bit more. Flight attendant staff moved about with a quickened pace. Engines changed their tone, clouds enveloped the plane and she rose and fell to turbulence. Absurdly proud of my biblical astuteness in the setting, I thought, " . . . and they were terrified as they entered the cloud" (Luke 9:34b), and grinned at my own pomposity.

The plane broke free of the erstwhile Cloud of Unknowing into partial sunshine, and began to bank. The pilot's voice crackled through the compartment, "There on your left, folks, is an unusual sight — London in the sunshine."

chapter 8

the welcome of columcille

To LOOK UPON LONDON from the air seemed impossibly exotic. From our height, I caught myself trying to see the kind of Victorian chimneypots that Mary Poppins wafted among, umbrella in hand. Nothing I saw actually looked like any stereotype I had of London. I turned my attention to the plane's landing, which afforded me another fine opportunity to get sweaty palms.

I felt a thrill of adventure mixed with anxiety as the plane rolled to the terminal. I thought with wonder: my first European airport.

I disembarked with a crush of people, my mumbly Spanish lady navigating to the fore. The airport teemed: hot, slightly sweaty. I had heard legends of how labyrinthine and confusing Heathrow was. Signs on the wall held some promise — international flights connecting domestically. That sounded right. I swung the brown backpack on my shoulder and began a distance-eating airport stride.

Halls, halls in Heathrow, all feeling not so much like Portland International but like the aged and over-used airports of New York. Discreet signs still pointed clearly but unobtrusively to "international flights connecting domestically." I walked and walked, round tight turns and down narrow staircases. Signs proudly boasted of the "new Heathrow renewal program," "making flight connection easier" in a hopeful sort of tone. If this was easy, I huffed to myself, the old Heathrow must have been a Hamster Habitrail, only without the cheese in the middle by way of reward.

I looked to my right and saw the mumbly Spanish lady working hard to keep up with me. I began to feel proprietary toward her, and as the airline list on the discreet signs included Iberia Airlines as well as my own, assumed the role of the blind leading the blind.

The narrow trails led to a kind of staging area, my first British "queue," with a young blond lady who somehow managed to be officious and polite at the same time. "Form a queue, then, right, and the tram will be here momentarily." I was absolutely tickled with her, "form a queue" and all!

A very British-looking little stocky bus-or-other arrived, and we managed to pile aboard quickly but with the utmost politeness. I continued to speak softly in Spanish to my mumbly Iberian lady, who looked more like a fish dumped from the water bowl minute by minute. The other passengers openly stared at the strange cross-cultural spectacle taking place before them. I for my part was having a great time.

When the growly little bus had snaked through some very dingy-looking industrial passages and ran under the tails of a lot of very exotically painted airplanes (like modern galleons, I thought), we arrived at last at another building with sooty glass walls, more distance to stride, more queues. "International arrivals" said the sign pointing us all up a set of escalators. By now, sweaty, we scanned signs that said things like "international passengers disembarking in Heathrow," "passengers connecting with international flights," "passengers connecting with domestic flights." I pointed my mumbly Iberian down her own stair, then got in my own "domestic connection" line. Behind me, I saw her standing, still confused, trying to get an additional clue from a bemused and not very patient-looking customs guard. He pointed her down a stair that I felt sure was incorrect and, slowly and heavily, the old dear heaved herself down and disappeared. I felt a pang of guilt that I didn't leap the barricade and catch her, try to get her pointed finally in the right direction. Although I'm sure that England and Spain put down their ancient Armada animosity long enough to set her straight and connect her with her family, I still worry about her.

The line separated us into "Non-Commonwealth" and "Commonwealth." I suddenly remembered how, as an American, I had been given preferential treatment in Japanese customs years ago while my fellow travelers from Korea got a rough going over. It was a strange relief to be the disenfranchised one and humbly wait on the longer line. People on the Commonwealth line seemed at ease and happy, chattering away. The Commonwealth line moved much more quickly, as well. The "Non" line inched slowly and unhappily in comparison.

The staff and officers I saw seemed to be mostly "Commonwealth" as well — many faces suggesting Asian roots, the accents a rich and charming mix of vast Asia and little England. They were calm and polite and very much in charge, unflappable in spite of the crush of people and the cloying heat which made sweat roll down many faces.

The rather bored fellow behind the counter seemed more the stereo-typical Anglo-Saxon Brit — "What, then, is your purpose in visiting the U.K.?" "Studies," I decided to tell them laconically. "Enjoy your stay, then," he said, placing a demure little stamp in my virginal passport. And grabbing my case off I walked down yet another stuffy corridor — a solitary Irish-American invasion of the heartland of southern England.

The corridor led me above a large open-air concourse, filled with rather expensive-looking shops. I recognized Harrods, but the rest were all new to me. A kind of fast-food pub looked promising, but at that point I only wanted to catch my plane. Besides, even though I was not yet used to British pounds, the prices looked atrocious. Airports are airports, after all.

The corridor finally turned and descended via a staircase to a set of cramped gates labeled "British Midlands." Turns out that I could have easily helped the mumbly Iberian lady — I could have escorted her to the English Channel and put her on a boat for Santiago de Compostela and still have made my plane. Stung by my lapse of basic charity in order to look after my own skin, I sat down, slightly dank with sweat.

I slung my bags under a chair and tried to unbend, unwind, and relax. I already felt weary and spent. But I was intensely curious about everything I saw.

What I found was an array of snacks for sale, lots of unappealing pastry-appearing things. I found, there in the departure gate, a sales stand with toiletry sorts of things as well as British pornography which, judging by the front covers, was a bit more frank than Yank varieties hidden behind wrappers on sale at airports. I gave the covers a long look and shook my head, not in disapproval but in foreboding of a month's worth of celibacy. I took my seat, and no, I didn't buy a magazine.

British Midlands flight attendants passed by, looking very natty in their blue bowler hats. If I had to draw a fantasy image of a British flight crew, that is how I would have dressed them.

The plane did not disappoint either. I was packed in beside some very resigned-seeming men with Scottish burrs, which they rarely exercised as they sat shyly in their seats. They seemed tired and their clothes suggested they were working-class men heading home for a bit. Another natty fellow, a slender young man who seemed quite harassed, bobbed back and forth asking, with exquisite politeness, "Would you like breakfast, then?" Determined that I was going to eat when I had the chance, drink when I had the chance, I said yes. The weary-looking men said no. They knew something I did not.

British Midlands is a charming and efficient airline, but all earthly things have their flaw. For British Midlands, it was their breakfast. A scorched plastic tray-plate arrived with a sort of egg-pastry concoction half-burned to the plastic. I think there were biscuits of some sort, and jam as well. I picked valiantly, not wanting to insult a whole airline on first encounter. The tired-looking men turned over to sleep, studiously avoiding so much as a glance at breakfast according to British Midlands. Indeed, they did know better.

The plane began to settle down to a landing in a green, grassy place surrounded by ancient-looking, stony hills. "Glasgow," intoned the intercom. As we touched down, further pleasantries were spoken electronically to us, to the effect that we had rejoiced their hearts by flying on British Midlands. I wondered if there is an airline that just tells you to get off the plane and get lost?

As I would several times on this voyage, I wished that there was someone waiting for me, dispelling the empty feeling of being the stranger at the airport. I walked purposefully enough, but slowed and stopped as I found a currency exchange booth. Nervously I stopped and rummaged through my things until I emerged with some traveler's checks. It was time to get some currency of the realm.

I love British money. It comes in tidy folds of paper, from differing banks, shot through with silver strands and in rich colors. The images are a public television tour of English history — kings and queens and even Robert the Bruce. I love British coins, especially the weighty, businesslike little pound coins. When you hold one, you feel the substance, and "sound as a pound" makes perfect sense. Immensely pleased that my pockets were now weighed down with pounds and pence, I continued on my way.

A nice lady with a charming burr (I fell in love with most Scottish women solely on the basis of voice) gave me a map and a ticket to the shuttle bus which would take me to downtown Glasgow and presumably to my hotel. The bus, a glass cube with a valiantly snarling motor, took me down what seemed to be endless highway ("motorway") into an area which looked like a dark concrete futuristic dream, *Modern Times* in gray. The taciturn but kind-seeming fellow let me off on an almost-deserted street lined with banks. "Right up the hill there, doon that street if ye don't want to walk so steep, oop that one if ye don't mind a wee climb." And the little glass cube snarled and scampered off.

I stood on the street of my first European city and wondered again just what I had gotten myself into.

I chose the wee climb. The one-page map told me which of the nearly vertical roads, lined with grim-looking buildings, led to the Theatre Hotel, my first stopping place. The wee climb with my small bags convinced me that I am in fact over forty, and British Midlands' breakfast gurgled at me merrily like an old but annoying acquaintance. Stopping at a corner, which seemed perched in the air after the climb, a wave of desolation swept over me. Alone in Glasgow, early enough in the morning that hardly a soul was visible, signs of urban decay sprinkled about, I felt utterly alien and alone, a core of loneliness in my soul swimming to the surface and filling my eyes with tears. It was all I could do to hold them back.

It wouldn't do to blubber on a Glasgow street corner, at least not yet. I picked up my bags and continued. I prayed in some wise, without words, laying my weary feet and my darkness of soul before heaven.

Outside of an ominous-looking dark brownstone church, done in a Gothic but Protestant style, I paused, panting. I glanced over at the sign on the side. A Gaelic blessing (presumably) was underscored by "St. Columcille and the Church of Scotland welcome you."

When one is a pilgrim, one becomes attuned to the signs and the graces that accompany the journey and through which heaven reaches out to the wanderer. Tears again stung my eyes, but tears of recognition and gratitude this time. The Celtic land and the Saint had opened their arms and bid me welcome.

chapter 9

glasgow,
the guilty pleasure

I FOUND THE THEATRE HOTEL, a charming place mid-street near to an actual theater. A lovely place reeking of atmosphere, the hotel was once a residence for actors and theater people going back two centuries and more. A lovely renovation has created modern guest rooms that are comfortable yet in keeping with the atmosphere. The common spaces preserve a sense of history. A front parlor looked just the right place to meet a bustled lady for tea, or to sip some porter while reading the Times of London. It's great when a place actually lives up to one's expectations! And no, they haven't paid me on commission.

The blue-eyed, round-faced young woman behind the desk, obviously very pregnant, opened her mouth to speak, and I fell in love again.

"You might walk aboot a bit, and visit the Cathedral and all. It's very nice."

I was exhausted but wide-awake and fidgety, and had no wish to lie about and miss anything. I threw a few things into my backpack and set out.

Glasgow's streets are bleak and gray, filled with a vital bustle of people, an energy that was heartening in spite of my tiredness and loneliness. I walked in wonder. Shops, even an elaborate-looking kiltmaker's — a name that I thought I remembered from Portland's Highland Games. Steep streets, cobbled. And ahead, just visible through the twists — the Cathedral.

"The Cathedral" hardly evokes the sense of awe I felt approaching the hoary, squat façade of what was obviously a very early Gothic stone structure. No lacy flying buttresses here — the building seems to crouch, heavy with history and Normans and Picts.

I was delighted with the place. I approached slowly, almost stalking it, walking in the outer yard crammed with tombs going back to the seventeenth century.

Inside was all busyness — students, tourists, well-dressed visitors filled the place. Some school class was obviously about some function or ceremony, all blues and plaids and blazers and skirts and energetic young faces. What looked like a chapter room close to the chancel was reserved for their affair.

I wended my way down to the crypt, about which I was silently corrected by a sign — "This is NOT called the crypt, but rather the 'lower cathedral.'"

A wonderful dark space was the not-crypt, partly kempt, partly a little neglected. Tombs and more tombs, statues and memorials. And at the center of the space was a stone block draped with a full frontal in rich colors, blue mostly, baroque and modern all at once. Over it hung a lovely oil lamp. In all directions chairs stood in small rows. In the chairs and, in some cases, on small kneelers, were people at prayer. Mostly young people, students in uniform of various sorts. A small sign proclaimed the block to be the tomb of St. Mungo. Mungo, Kentigern, fourth-century monk and contemporary of old Ninian down at his little White House, his Candida Casa by the Solway Firth. A true Old One, breathing his own dust there at the heart of the massive medieval cathedral, which was built six centuries after the frail fact that was Mungo's earthly life. I trembled, knelt, my eyes shifting from the lit oil lamp to the still shrouded block beneath. I don't remember words — sometimes just kneeling down in exhausted awe is prayer enough.

As discreetly as I could, I asked one tall young lass as she rose to go, "Do the Catholics come down here to pray before the saint?"

She looked a bit startled, but said, "We all do. He's the saint of the city."

"Are there usually so many during the week?"

"It's the exams," she said matter-of-factly.

When sectarian arguments are all said and done, at Mungo's tomb Protestants and Catholics will pray together for good exams. In a polemic world, it's one of the most hopeful things I've seen of late.

The galleries of ancient tombs and slabs dedicated to the great and probably not-so of old Scotia were perfect. I wandered happily in that gallery of the dead.

Outside, the day bright but windy and chill, the grim cathedral square was filled with running, chatting, vibrant Scottish schoolchildren, teenagers in blazers and slacks and tartan skirts. I almost expected the school patches to say "Hogwarts," but not everything lives up to fantasy, after all. At this point in my journey I was prepared to be charmed by everything. And so I was.

Nearby buildings seemed to be vaguely tourist-oriented. Upstairs in one as I roamed, I found display cases with wooden images. A few were delightfully otherworldly and probably pre-Christian, with bulging eyes and bold priapic penises. "Found in a bog," said the label laconically, leaving viewers to draw their own conclusions.

Others possessed the same bulbous eyes and exaggerated heads, but were more modest and more intentionally Christian with cross-motifs. There were abbot's crosiers and reliquaries. I gaped at the sort of objects that I had previously seen only in pictures. Again I was delighted, but also a powerful melancholy fell over me — in the heart of a tough industrial town, the scraps of the ancient Celtic past looked forlorn and anachronistic. Was this a fool's errand, chasing Celtic ghosts that the world had left behind? I began to tremble with sheer weariness and worried about getting back to the hotel without collapsing.

But I breathed deeply and walked slowly and made my way back. I forsook with reluctance the Necropolis, the wonderfully macabre collection of tombs and mausoleums filling the hillside overlooking the Cathedral, which came to be during a past era of plague. The Necropolis is clearly a part of Glasgow's daily thoroughfares, as I saw students and younger children scampering up its grim streets laughing. My Gothic tastes love places like this, so only my trembling and the thought that if I pushed I might be apartment-hunting on that sepulchral street drove me back home.

Home, in Glasgow . . . I roamed its bustling, energized, rugged streets with delight. I found a somewhat hip pub that sold me bangers and mash and a decent pint for about four pounds. I found a teeming bookstore in which a freckly little girl ran up to me and skidded to a stop and smiled, then turned away shyly as if I had done the running. I smiled at her and at her pretty freckly mom and was enchanted with them as soon as they spoke. It became quite exhausting emotionally. I walked and walked, and was taken for a local by a tall and slender Asian student who needed directions and looked very stressed and in a great hurry. I shared my sketchy knowledge of the surrounding five blocks and wished her well. And I loved Glasgow. It's almost a guilty pleasure, as when I tell Scottish-knowledgable people this they immediately say, "Oh, well Glasgow . . . Did you get to Edinburgh? I *really* loved Edinburgh, you've got to see it. . . . " But Glasgow, you have my love I say, and I thank you for welcoming me home.

I had a solid day or so of walking, of listening, of going to sleep exhausted at 5 PM and waking at 11 PM Scottish time. But Glasgow and the Theatre Hotel were a good place in which to recover from jet-lag.

I wrote, "Feelings heightened. When I miss Dina and the kids, I *ache*. When I'm moved, tears spring. When I'm speaking to a person, I'm *enchanted*. I gain a sense of my own worth and preciousness. People who love and respect me wanted me to make this trip!"

But loving and leaving Glasgow were both necessary. I bought a phone card, having learned that the squat beige pay-phones in the British Isles well earn their nickname of "one-armed bandits." They eat pound coins and belch, demanding more. I called and made a reservation at a B&B in a tiny town called Fionnphort, pronounced "Fin-fert." It lies on the end of Mull, the larger island which overlooks Iona. It was a shot in the dark, making the reservation, but I had a feeling that contemplating Iona awhile before setting foot on it would be important. I did not know how true that was to be.

chapter 10

of ferries and trains and fires

THERE ARE TWO train stations in Glasgow, let the traveler beware, and they're not close by one another. It's not unusual to have to make a connection between the two, and the cabbies must make a fortune shuttling madly between them with frantic passengers gaping at their watches.

There were many tracks, but clearly marked trains, clean and colorful and efficient. I easily found mine and found a car with seating. I heaved my swollen brown backpack and compact little green case aboard, not for the last time regretting not paying out for one large pack and a money belt. I'm glad I escaped arrest over there for public indecency, periodically grabbing my right cheek to make sure the wallet still rode there secure. Buy the belt, people — it saves grief.

A nice Glasgow couple, togged up in sturdy-looking outdoor clothes and maneuvering bicycles on board, shyly struck up a conversation. "You on holiday, then?" I allowed as I was "on holiday," and they proceeded to casually do a marvelous job as tour-guides, both of the land and of the landscape of the souls of a couple of average Scottish folks. Harry and Fiona — childless couple, free spirits, taking a bike trip with the help of many ferries through the Outer Hebrides. A pilgrimage indeed, albeit with little overt religiosity. In fact, Fiona assured me, they themselves were "not religious," but they had a friend who was a Church of Scotland minister. He and his wife had been living on Iona in the abbey as members of the Iona Community, and had had a baby there. Living with the baby at the abbey was not easy, she allowed — the community "had trouble handling it." Now they lived in Glasgow, still affiliated with the community.

Harry was the more loquacious of the two — after a bit Fiona withdrew, and I sensed she wanted Harry to herself. But first she pointed out a few scrubby trees dotting the hillside. "All that's left," she said, "of the Caledonian Forest." Images of Roman cavalrymen up from Hadrian's Wall chasing after blue-painted Picts filled my mind. "And down there, of course, is Loch Lomond." Of course. "Rob Roy was from around here, and there, and over there." I asked if they realized how they lived in a land which was, for us, a land of legend. "Ah weel, we feel that way about the States, now." Touché.

Harry wanted to see my maps, and we pored over them. They told me how to keep fumbling my way to Iona through the Highlands, and especially how to manage when I found myself at the water's edge.

And we did find ourselves at the water's edge, as the train pulled into Oban, or as I tried to say, "OOOOO-bin." I stumbled after Harry and Fiona as they wheeled their bicycles, tick tick tick, out the doors and across the tracks. I resisted the needy impulse to cling to them — after all, Fiona needed some time with Harry, and my pride wanted me to feel capable of finding my own way, albeit with the kindness of strangers.

The smell of salt air made me feel at home. The ferry window staff was patient and polite in telling me just when the ferry to Mull would arrive and where it would go. I bought a ticket and set myself to find some lunch.

A wonderful unpretentious shack sold sandwiches right there at the dock. A few pounds got you your choice of salmon or prawn, and a cup of scalding tea. I recommend them both. I still don't know why the tea tastes so good over there.

The ferry arrived, a big businesslike ship filled with people and cars. I stood and took my place in the queue, an amazing crush of humanity and careful, slightly edgy politeness. Disembarking folks were mostly greeted by people who knew them and gathered them in their arms. Not for the first time I felt the aloneness of the stranger, as I turned away from simple human warmth and explored the ship.

I am accustomed to ferries since I grew up on Long Island and loved to take the grunting, rusting ships from Port Jefferson to Bridgeport, Connecticut. This ship was newer, bigger, somehow more businesslike, as if people depended on it for daily commutes and not for recreation. On board were small shops and food places (open) and, beer taps (unfortunately closed).

Even though a bit of rain was splatting and spraying fitfully between clouds and sun-breaks, I chose the outside deck. The sights and the Scottish wind were intoxicating and not to be missed.

Having placed its human and mechanical cargo in its belly like some enormous, unsentimental mothering creature, the ship backed from port with the deepest of grunts and growls and, pointing to the harbor mouth, slowly got underway. A creamy wake grew and pointed to where we had been.

Oban began to recede from the ship's rail. From the water I found the port beautiful. I saw picturesque docks and town buildings, on the hilltop a "folly," an attempt on the part of some local moneyed gentry to build a Coliseum-like monument. A lovely ruined castle at the harbor mouth — sea-tolls must have been lucrative during the feudal extortion of the Middle Ages. A neat lighthouse stood at the point, and to finish it all nicely a lovely rainbow.

I leaned over the rail and drank it in. I loved it and ached for my wife's hand in mine as we would show each other the sights and drink the clean air.

A slightly built, forthright woman walked up to me and asked me to take her picture in front of the lovely rainbow. Bemused, I did so, then asked her to reciprocate. I learned she was a Yank, and as it turned out from Seattle. A pilgrim, as she later told me, bound for Iona for the second time. It felt good to talk to another pilgrim and to a woman. Paradoxically it comforted me and drove home my aloneness at one and the same time. On pilgrimage I often felt keenly two or more contrasting emotions at the same time. Or was it just that I paid more attention than I do on ordinary days?

I communed silently with the God of pilgrims, as much as I could, while the gray water, quicksilver-light and filled with legend, slid smoothly past.

The Isle of Mull, ancient isle of stories including Robert Louis Stevenson's tale of the kidnapped young lad, drew near, patient and dark green and large before the prow. We docked in Craignuire. Buses awaited those who walked with purpose to them, dragging their luggage, as well as for those who, like me, stumbled clueless and confused.

The bus easily swallowed our luggage, which the stoic Scottish driver slung and stacked in its capacious underbelly. I quizzed the poor patient fellow anxiously — did the bus go to Fionnphort? "Aye," he assured me, "Aye, right there, after a wee drive aboot the island and hoping the sheep don't make for a longer trip." I took my seat, wondering how mutton could be a factor in travel time.

The bus was not very full at all. Joanie, my Seattle pilgrim acquaintance, got on and, much more at ease than I, struck up a conversation with a shy young woman and her little girl. I just sat and stared out the window.

The scenery of the island was harsh and stark, searing yet green and verdant at once, a secret and stubborn fertility wrested from ancient rocks. The timeless bones of the land, powerful remorseless stone, thrust up through the lowest of moss and what I later learned was Scottish heather. The land was alive, primordially alive, and redolent of magic and ancient memory. I fully understood the word "bewitched" that day. The wise, ancient land was placing me under its spell.

And that was as well, because the journey was longer, because of the mutton factor.

Small, energetic brown sheep with velvety black faces were everywhere. They clambered over rock, gathered in small clumps tearing at the tough sparse growth, darted like sturdy minnows adapted to land. When they moved with cocky impunity into the road, the driver slowed, honked, and often came to a complete stop. Radical mutton right-of-way is strictly observed in Scotland. And so there was plenty of time to feast the eyes on the land, to drink in the sparse gray light, as sparse as the low heather and moss gathered about the rocks like water gathered about islands. Like a Zen garden, the landscape invited thought.

I wrote, "Bare green — nothing to excess or cloaking that which is true. What is true is earth, light, water, people, air — the very life lived.

Jesus said 'Leave all and follow me.' Columba heard that call. It brought
him here. Where will I go, where will I be led?"

The bus arrived when it arrived and not a minute before, in Fionnphort, tiny hamlet perched on the edge of a small strait. The village
seemed to arrange and define itself as a way-station, with a parking lot
and the concrete ferry ramp central to all. Small neat white houses,
immaculate. Meticulously tended yards, no fences. A tiny park area, a
sitting place really, with a bench and small table and carefully cultivated
grassland. Across the road and down a slope was a small cemetery. A
lift of the eyes and a look into the sunset revealed the end, the goal, the
holy isle.

Iona. It lay in the west like a dream, a mirage. In the setting sun
could clearly be seen the squat brown tower and roof line of the restored
Benedictine priory. Near enough to touch, yet existing on the edge of
dream, not of this world.

I had checked the ferry schedule and realized that there were still a
couple of runs left that day. I could scuttle over to Iona if I wished. But I
found I did not wish so. I do not know why, but it seemed to me wise to
long for the island first, to stop poised on its borders and keep in touch
with the longing in my heart.

I remembered the words of my friend which had moved me so. "Brigid
and Columba want you to come home for awhile."

Almost home, Abba, I thought silently, moving my lips when I
thought the words.

I checked into a B&B right up the street from the ferry. I explored
Fionnphort, which did not take very long. The cemetery drew me, and
as I entered a flight of ravens rose in the air, wheeled, and swept over me.
Have a care, the spirits are near, their ebony wings seemed to whisper.
I walked contentedly among the graves: some more than a century old,
others quite recent. So-and-so, "the Ferryman of Iona." I walked and
prayed for all who lay here, who had called this small, sacred spot their
home, who had lived and died and seen all weathers from these stones,
this heather.

I found safe refuge in a snug pub, stone-walled and wooden-floored.
Plenty of seating, so I took one next to the peat fire, its slightly iodine

aroma a romantic comfort. I settled in with a good pint of bitters and a spot of food. Lots of visitors walked in and out, and lots of locals too, hard-working folks in soiled clothes, greeting each other with shouts and easy joy at the end of the day. I liked them — it was easy to like them. I nursed the pint and wrote, "It doesn't get much better this side of the Final Coming."

The last light of the dying day lit the tops of Iona's hills as I gazed out the window of my bedroom. Iona lay gilded, crowned with light fleeting yet eternal, indomitable. I stared until my eyes ached, until the light died altogether and the island lay hidden, cloaked in darkness, yet still powerfully present, a reality and even a consciousness on the other edge of sight. I shuddered and closed the window.

chapter 11

holy isle of the west

T HE NEXT DAY DAWNED chill and clear. I arose and packed, feeling
nervous, as if I were scheduled to meet someone famous. On some
level I feared making a fool of myself, but with whom I was not sure.

I had a fine B&B breakfast ("Will you have the Scottish breakfast?
Or the kippers, then?"). The friendly, capable young couple who owned
the place spoke of their life without much urging. The husband works
with his wife at the B&B, and also "works at the fishing." Speaking with
them was one of the moments when prowling among old stones and
communing with those long dead stood in contrast with those who work
and play and laugh and raise their kids and grow old amidst those stones
and the dead today. I wondered, brooding over my kippers, about those
who come in turn to the U.S.A., looking for a romantic past or some
quintessential American experience. How we long for something other
than our own place! How far we will journey from the place and people
that made and shaped us in order to find out who we truly are!

I paid my tab and bid my hosts farewell, not without regret. That
B&B was a comfortable place, and it was tempting to just stay on to
rest. But the isle was already calling, tapping its foot.

I trotted down through a bit of splattery rain to the tiny ferry station
in time to see the ferry, boxy to the point of being a seagoing cube,
bustling up to the concrete ramp. It let down its gate, and a car emerged
and climbed past. A few people emerged as well, casually avoiding the
seawater washing over the ramp and looking for all the world like a
careless sort of understaffed amphibious invasion, one peaceful enough
to excite no resistance. I timed the little waves and walked over the
steel ramp into the ferry's bowels. I climbed a stair out of the car-bay,

and so found myself in a windowed cabin, with benches and the now-familiar Caledonian-MacBray ferry company signs proclaiming "fast and safe service to all the Scottish islands."

The ferry grunted and shoved itself into the sound. As its momentum increased and the bow-wave grew, Iona drew nearer. I drew a shuddering breath.

Something large in my pocket poked my thigh. I reached in and withdrew the key to the B&B. I smiled. Columba was having some fun with me, telling me to lighten up. All the holy archetypes come along on pilgrimage — the sage, the prophet, the priest, the shaman, the warrior, the king/queen — but most definitely the trickster-fool. I greeted him silently and told him ruefully I'd try to not take myself so damned seriously.

Iona grew from the water like a dream. I wrote, "Lovely small houses, all browns and grays. The windswept short green of the grass. The restored Benedictine Abbey waited, sharp peaked roof lines and severe square tower, patient and seeming eternal."

As the ferry made land and the gate was lowered, I could clearly see the long low building with its prominent sign — the Argyll Hotel, where our seminar group was to stay. A wooden pushcart was waiting at the ferry marked with the same name in a Celtic uncial script, but I elected to walk and carry my own gear. Only a few steps down the lane of cottages brought me to the hotel's door.

The Argyll proved to be a marvelous old, narrow, twisty place, architecture way too old to have heard of feng shui or "flow." I found its labyrinth-like hallways, small doorways, and tiny parlors with burning peat fires living up to any romantic Scottish image that I ever had. It used to be the village inn. I wished the walls could talk. Or not, I corrected myself, shuddering, as Scotland is quite famous for its ghost stories and I thought I was far too busy to be distracted with a haunting in my room.

Lovely young Scottish women showed me to my room. Again, I fell in love as soon as they opened their mouths and spoke. My inner adolescent was getting worn out with one-minute-long crushes on Scottish women based on their speech, so I thanked them hurriedly and stowed my gear.

The room was small, just a place to sleep really, clean and austerely elegant.

I called the B&B in Fionnphort, and Nancy, the owner, told me to give the key to the ferry captain. I marveled at the easy cooperation of those who make a living on these isles, as I climbed to the bridge of the just-returned ferry. The captain accepted the key with the briefest of explanations from me, and chugged away as soon as I debarked.

I wrote, "Then I was free, and the spirit of the place gathered close around."

I wanted to meet Iona, the ancient Iona. I got almost more than I bargained for.

This portion is hard for me to write, although in intensity of experience other moments rivaled it — Glendalough, Kildare. I think imagination and longing and openness and the answer to pilgrim prayer all conspired to grant me a deep engagement with these holy places, places that belong to all the world and all humanity. It's part of the strange magic of pilgrimage that sacred places hallowed by God and so many hearts and hands and weary feet afford a deep personal encounter to those who come as seekers. I was very blessed. The encounter cannot be forced. It is always a grace and a gift.

I walked slowly, as in a dream, south past a pub, past the first Celtic cross I saw — a relatively new one, a memorial to the twentieth-century war dead of the island.

Every tiny bit of Iona, every hillock and hummock, every bit of beach and pile of stones, has a name and a story and is woven into the sacred geography of the island. Every bit is soaked with history, and not all by any means sweetness and light. Darkness and murder and shadow play freely on Iona as well as grace and glory, shifting just beneath the thin veil of the surface of the Now. All make an ever-pulsing Celtic knotwork that can draw in and envelop the pilgrim. Drink deep, traveler, but walk with care.

Past the war memorial was a tiny curve of beach, white sand ending in a little headland on which was a large house. By its high-peaked roof and its small bell tower it was clear that it was a converted church. I knew the beach from reading and, well, from just knowing: Martyr's Bay.

Depending on whom you ask, Martyr's Bay is one of the sites where Iona monks were slaughtered by Viking raiders, or the landing where novice candidates for the monastery would arrive from Mull and first touch the sacred isle, or the place where the dead, Christian and pre-Christian Druidic both, would be ferried from Mull to begin their interment on Iona the western isle of the dead and of eternal life, Tir Na N'Og. I stood and reveled at the unresolved, interwoven stories. All that needs to be true is that the little beach is a portal, an entryway, hallowed by pilgrim feet and the thin veil between life and death. I looked around to see if I was being observed. I had a sense that someone just might be watching curiously from the former church, but I shrugged. I had come so far, and was not going to let embarrassment dictate what I would do this day. Lowering myself prone on the beach, face down, I kissed the sands and arose with Iona clinging to my lips. The sand was fine and slightly sweet. Tiny waves lapped a ceaseless, merry music. I waited for one of the waves and scooped up a palm full of the clear salt water, touched my tongue to it, laved my forehead and blessed myself with it as with holy water, and shuddered with delight as the water trickled down my cheeks and neck, wetting my collar. Tears stung my eyes as I recited from memory the Te Deum, the ancient church's hymn of praise. The sun broke from clouds and shone bright upon the beach. I prayed for all martyrs then and now, for forgiveness for the roistering old savage Vikings who carved the "blood-eagle" upon monkish backs, forgiveness for all oppressors and for those who visit violence and misery upon the helpless and vulnerable. I prayed for justice. My heart and my head pounded.

I do not know how long I stood at Martyr's Bay. Time stopped that day, or rather time was not as time usually is.

Holy places tell you clearly without words when it is time to move on. As Joanie, my fellow Northwestern pilgrim, told me with wisdom born of experience, one must not be greedy with the holy places. We receive what we need and nothing more.

I somehow knew when to lift my feet and begin to walk, back up the lane, away from the bay and back into the tiny village. Before me

loomed the beautiful red stone ruins of what a sign declared was "The
Nunnery."

A medieval Augustinian priory of women, the Augustinian "Nunnery" was founded at about the same time as the Benedictine priory
up the road. Both of these continental European monastic orders, high
medieval imports to the British Isles, had hit upon a brilliant piece of
public relations. They deliberately chose to settle on Iona so as to bask in
and take on the ancient holiness and reputation of Columba's old Celtic
monastic community. It is unclear whether there were still Celtic monks
present on Iona when the new monks and nuns came. We'll never know
if the old monastery's memory was still carried by actual Celtic monks
or if all that remained was oral tradition passed on by the inhabitants of
the island. But then, anyone living on Iona at the time could be considered members of the Iona monastic community or descended from it.
In Iona's great days the community was the island, the island was the
community — no distinction was made as would be made today with the
tidier monks with their property lines and signs and fences. Any islander,
of either gender and any state of life, would have been considered one
of the *manaig,* observing a form of the community's Rule and both con-
tributing to and benefiting from its life. I hope that anyone remaining
on the isle who preserved its old identity was treated with respect by the
newcomers, but the Middle Ages were a time of even less respect for
religious differences than is our own intolerant age.

I walked slowly into the lovely ruins open to the sky, "lovely bones"
indeed, through which a tended path threaded, a path I later learned
had been hacked by one of the Dukes of Argyll to make a walking path
for his guests. Wildflowers bloomed, bravely nodding in the breeze.

The layout of medieval "conventual" monasteries is pretty uniform
and not so different from such monasteries today. I approached the out-
line of a square room still lined with stone benches. The sisters' chapter
room for sure, I thought, where they would meet daily for work assign-
ments and for conferences with the abbess. I stood in the remains of the
doorway and most surely in my mind's eye the sisters were there, black-
clad in rows on the benches. They looked up and I shuddered, then

smiled. I was welcome there, so long as I did not forget my courtesy. Wordlessly I asked their leave, and the sisters assented with a nod.

A gull wheeled over the remains of the refectory, crying and seeming to mourn the long-dead nuns. But he had more than medieval nuns to mourn. This land was old before Columba, old even before the Celts. Its bones are laved with ancient and primal holiness, the holiness of creation itself. Geologists say that Iona's rock is, among the stuff of earth, truly ancient. Storytellers say that Iona was split off from the first strong foundation that God brought forth from chaos. On Iona, at least, the scientists and the storytellers agree.

I emerged from the convent ruins and walked slowly up the lane. Foot traffic was sparse — not too many day-trippers, the folks the Beatles sang about and who are both the profit and the regret of island folk. To this day they debate the marketing of Iona as a "religious theme park." Late September is a good time to be on the island — businesses and accommodations still open, weather still clear at times, solitude easy to come by.

As I walked, the voices of the island beat about my ears, loud, at times a sustained roar heard not with the ears but with the mind. I felt afraid, and yet at the same time felt more at home than I had anywhere else for a long time.

The path turned right, and I followed. The path wound gently, oddly familiar.

At a bend I met an older standing Celtic stone cross. MacLean's Cross, the sign said. Not the most ancient, but handsome and intricately carved. I knelt in prayer, taking off my battered black cap. I stood, and continued.

I remembered reading the old dictum of the pilgrim to Iona, of those who sought St. Columba's blessing and a favor from the intercession of the saint. To be heard by St. Columba, go first to St. Oran.

According to several stories, Oran was one of Columba's original companions. Upon landing on Iona, Columba declared that the Lord had told him that one of their number would have to consent to death in order to make firm the foundation of their new home. In this story is a powerful echo of Columba's Druidic roots and the free interplay of Christian and pre-Christian elements in the early Christianity of the isles. The Celts as well as many other peoples of the time completed the foundation of new buildings by sacrifice, the blood of the victim soaking the stones and the strength of the spirit of the victim binding all together and pleasing the gods. Animals would do for small private houses, humans for great buildings. Who knows if this story recounts an actual human sacrifice performed, or if the more pious account that Oran offered himself to God and then died at God's own hand is somehow true, or if Oran died shortly after Columba's debarking and his death was subsequently understood by Druidic-formed Christians as the necessary sacrifice? The story is grim in any telling, and if nothing else speaks of the suffering and death of that age, of the fate of the vulnerable, of the "otherness" of God's realm and God's thought, and of how loss and blood can be found even at the gates of grace.

However the story was in reality, St. Columba was said to say to Oran before his death, "No one who comes to me with a petition will be heard, unless he come first to you."

One comes to Oran in his sacred place: the ancient cemetery, Reilig Odhrain, St. Oran's Churchyard.

The tiny, bumpy cemetery, no perfect manicured symmetric suburban graveyard this, pulsed silently with the vigor of its ancient holy dead. The graves — so many and so close by one another. Stones of all ages, some tiny, some small because of wear. Many missing, I later learned, taken to the abbey as monuments to be displayed and thus frustrating the efforts of scholars to identify the graves and study the whole. Monks and laity, kings and queens, graves from the age of Shakespeare's MacBeth among them, as well as the recently dead John Smith, the Scottish politician and leader who is still mourned and regretted, all there and all together. Iona is the Champion's Portion of the dead, the honor among honors in Scotland given as a hero's farewell.

I threaded my way through the graves to the simply oblong oratory, St. Oran's Chapel. The oldest standing building on the island still in use, St. Oran's dates from the eleventh century and can be said to be from the late "Celtic" period.

Inside I found a living place of prayer. A tender, naïve little icon of a child lay propped at the feet of a concrete altar. An iron circular candle stand, filled with tea light candles, stood in one corner near the door. Standing behind it was a crude wooden cross, with petitions hand-written on paper and tacked on. Its simplicity reminded me suddenly of Mexican and Filipino shrines and *votos* pinned onto the drapery of statues and holy images in Hispanic lands. My father-in-law, who had died the previous summer, suddenly felt very present, and I welcomed him and let him see this holy place through my eyes.

I wrote my own petition and tacked it on:

> Renewal and healing for the parish,
> Joy and security for my family,
> That I might seek first the kingdom of God.

I knelt and prayed my heart out to God and to Saint Oran.

There are sudden, dread moments, graced and awe-filled, when one senses that one's prayer has been heard in the depths of God. I shuddered as I rose, knowing that my prayer had been heard.

I touched my rosary to the altar, and said my farewell.

God in his mercy gave me breaks during this day, else I wonder if I would have died outright or lost some measure of my sanity. I am quite serious about that. I felt utterly hedged about and experienced wonder, joy, love, fear, tears all at once. The road on which I walked was crowded, even though I could see no one.

Out the Reilig Odhrain and to the abbey gates, a sign told me of a ticket that I would need to buy. I wandered across the road to what proved to be the Iona Community's bookshop. Turns out there was no ticket to be had there — in a casual Celtic trusting gesture, one has to enter deep within the abbey to an undercroft shop to buy said ticket. Entering deep within to gain the right of entry is a parable in itself, but by then I was getting punchy with parables and I shook off further ruminations.

I walked slowly into the abbey grounds. Ahead stood the great High Crosses, two intact and one only a base with fragments. To the left, a small stone outcrop about fifteen feet high — Tor Abb, the Abbot's Hill,

by tradition the site of Columba's cell within the *vallum* or earthwork
wall of the monastic enclosure. Not for me, yet. I slowly approached
high, slim St. Martin's Cross, bowed, knelt, and prayed. The intricacy
of the dynamic Celtic knot-work pulsed, the carved biblical figures still
visible. Standing, my feet slipped slightly. Looking down, I saw a wide
winding path of large round stones leading from the walls of St. Oran's
Churchyard. My heart leaped, the metal taste of fear in my mouth. I had
read of this road — the Street of the Dead. Pilgrim's path to Columba's
cell, way that the corpses would be born for blessing and burial, way I
think as well that the spirits pass in ceaseless pilgrimage through the thin
place which is Iona.

Afraid I'd been unintentionally rude, I walked quickly along the west
side of the road to St. Oran's wall. Then I turned with rosary in hand.
Praying the "Jesus Prayer," "Lord Jesus Christ, have mercy on me," I
walked the Street of the Dead.

My feet slipped and turned. It is not easy to walk the pilgrim's way.
It is not easy to walk at all. What matters, on the Street of the Dead as
well as in life, is that one keeps walking.

They thronged about me, all the pilgrims — so many. They thronged
about me, the dead whose spirits move along that road each night to
pass before the abbot's cell for his blessing. They pressed upon me. My
heart constricted in my chest and my head pounded again. Reaching the
end of the Street, I was almost too dizzy to stand.

I stumbled back to the high crosses. I placed my hand holding the
rosary on the stump of St. Matthew's. I felt an oath coming on, but it
seemed impertinent to swear by Christ's blood as I was first moved to do.
Rather, I swore by my own blood, asking as well Jesus' grace to enable
me to bring my wife here to see what I was seeing that day.

My prayer was heard.

I stood and was at a loss. I tried the main great door of the church. I
am so used to locked church doors in the States that I was surprised to
find this one opening easily to the twist of my hand.

Inside the well-restored, austere church, a service was in progress.
Very Calvinist in tone it was, attended by nice-looking middle-aged Scottish people. I thought God and the saint wanted me to rejoin the living

for a bit. I sat down, soul aching, grateful for the respite. I found myself praying fearfully that I would keep my feet on the ground.

After the service, I poked about the church for a bit. A side window depicted Brigid — I was *so* glad to see her, a familiar face in a strange place! Effigies of the last abbots of Iona, including the Abbot Dominic whom Philip Sheldrake in *Living Between Worlds* reports had two sons and a daughter! Ostentatious carved marble effigies of a Duke and Duchess of Argyll lay in one ornate alcove, looking anachronistic and out of place.

I found the shop and bought a ticket. "Good all day," the nice Scottish man who sold me it assured me. He then told me to "walk right in to Columba's shrine." On pilgrimage, one must pay attention to those who are guardians of the gates.

Out the main abbey door and right, I ducked and entered a small, low doorway with a pointing sign, "St. Columba's Shrine."

I had arrived at last — the first ending of my journey. I knelt and bowed my head low. Tears sprang to my eyes. I took out the little book of intercessions from parish members and laid it down on the stones. A wooden crozier stood in a corner. A contemporary wooden cross inlaid with an image of Columba was affixed to the wall.

Unashamed, I spoke from my heart to the saint. I prayed for the world, the parish, my family, myself.

And my prayer was heard.

I stumbled out into the light of day. Within was still the pulsing sense of the saint's presence, slowly fading. But on Iona, as elsewhere, Columba is not to be found solely in his shrine.

Before me was the Tor Abb. I stood at its foot, feeling the other pilgrims invisible around me, and saluted the abbot at his cell.

I was invited up the hill. In joy and fear, I climbed. A clear path threaded its way up the Tor, between stones and heather and moss.

I stood at the top, at the lip of the stone circle, perhaps the foundation of his ancient cell within the enclosure. In my mind's eye, he stood and greeted me.

My throat caught as I asked him to be my soul-friend, my *anamchara.* He assented.

I turned and descended, walked slowly away across the Street of the Dead. My head was by now splitting with pain, and dizziness made walking difficult. I knew it was time to leave. But I walked away in grace. And, his company strange but assuring, an old one walked with me, his abbot's staff rapping strongly on the hardened ground.

I returned to the hotel and, finding my room, slept deeply and dreamlessly for hours.

chapter 12

BARÐS anÐ VISIONS

I MET TWO MEN walking slowly in the village later that day, possessed of leisurely purpose. One was Bob Wilhelm, a dignified man projecting an inner gravitas. Bob and his talented spouse, Kelly, are founders of Storyfest Ministries, teachers of the power of sacred storytelling and encouraging its practice in the ministries of the Church as well as in the larger world.

Our seminar convened that night in the Argyll. I was very pleased by the seminar participants. They included a charming pair of Dominican nuns, a Franciscan priest who proudly sported a kilt and sporran, a therapist couple from Missouri, and an Episcopalian couple. Most were veterans of previous storytelling pilgrimages. The group was engaging, warm, and trusting.

Guides, chosen or discovered by chance, are deeply important on pilgrimage. The Wilhelms were marvelous guides to the spiritual geography of Iona as well as to the geography drawn upon the soul by story. The time on Iona was made infinitely richer thanks to their kind guidance and care.

Bob and Kelly encouraged us to attend services at Iona Abbey. I did so once, and was not sorry. The Communion service was simple and moving. There was nothing outstanding — no wondrous preaching, no entrancing music — just a body of folk at prayer and glad to be there, glad to be praying. The eucharistic bread, good heavy oat-bread, was passed from hand to hand along with earthenware chalices of wine. At the end of the service small oak-cakes were passed around and we were invited to share half "with someone you don't know."

"Coffee hour," the socializing which is half of the service in many a church, took place in the abbey cloister. There were many living people

to speak to, while we were surrounded by grave-slabs from the Reilig
Odhrain hanging from the walls. The stones seem to lean in and be glad
of the conversation and of the life. I broke my little cake and shared it
with a pleasant young Irishman named Barry — I'm afraid I became a bit
emotional when it hit me that I was speaking to one of "my people," my
mother's people, an Irishman on the isle where Columba the Irishman
had made his exile's home. Barry told me he had been on a "spiritual
search" since the '70s, which had led him to the Focolare movement in
Italy. He had been affiliated with Focolare, a lay Roman Catholic society,
ever since. His transparency moved me.

I drifted back into the abbey church and found a set of stone stairs
winding to a tiny, low-ceilinged space right over Columba's tiny chapel-
shrine, which in turn is placed over what is thought to be the site of
Columba's first grave. I could think of no use for the small space except
as a kind of private place of prayer, a desert-nook or cave, as you will. I
sat within it for a little while, and wrote and prayed.

Later, Bob guided us to the top of the height called Cnoc Mor. He
told us that this was the site of Columba's old *diseart* or desert-place
of solitude. In Adomnan's ancient biography, Columba is described as
often seeking solitude, looking across from his retreat to present-day
Fionnphort where pilgrims would call for a boat to bring them to Iona.
Bob and I searched and found what we thought were the faint round
remains of the foundation of a stone hut, right on the peak. I stood and
thought that I understood Columba right well — he'd climb so that he
could get clear of the community and their incessant "Father, father!"
requests. From there he could get some peace, from there he could look
down on the goings-on, shake his head, and ask God just what God had
gotten him into and just what was he to do with those bloody monks
anyhow. Some things do not change.

Looking around 360 degrees, Bob asked us to notice that the shape
of Iona is remarkably similar to the shape of Ireland as a whole. He said
that the early Iona community was probably quite aware of this, and
that they kept the ancient four-part division of Ireland in mind as they
ordered their common life. In the center of the isle as in the center
of old Ireland was the ruling place, the monastery behind its earthen

vallum wall just as in Ireland's center is Leinster with its ancient royal district of Meath, the place of the High King. In the north of old Ireland was Ulster, the warrior place, the abode of the great and homicidal hero Chu Chulainn and the cycle of stories about him and the Red Branch Knights. For the Iona monks, the island's north was the place of testing and of ordeal. Their imagery of monastic life was that of the warrior, and Columba himself was called by Adomnan his biographer an "island soldier." Novices and penitents were set to ordeals in the north of the island, on the Hill of the Seat as well as at other sites. Here the monks would learn to be spiritual warriors, and here they fled during the first Viking raid on the island. Bob speculated that they fled north to partake of the warrior spirit that dwelled there, to turn and fight or to face their deaths like warriors of God. And there they died, on the small lugubrious stretch of beach called the White Strand of the Monks.

In the south of Ireland lies Munster, place of work and labor. There perhaps dwelt on Iona the crofters and laborers, as well as the women, although a small desolate island in the sound is called Eilean Nam Ban, the Women's Isle. Perhaps the Iona monks were not as whole and integrated and at ease between the genders as our romantic hopes would like. One tradition says that Columba exiled all women from the island, even the female animals, just like Mount Athos in Greece does today. But other stories speak of nuns on the island and of a conversation with an old woman that Columba shared in the Reilig Odhrain. Then, of course, the Augustinian nuns lived there in later years.

In the west of Ireland lies Connaght, beautiful yet harsh, the place of mystic vision, partaking of the sacrality that the West connotes for the Celtic soul. It's also a place of testing — "To Hell or to Connaght" was the harsh choice given by the English to Irish rebels. Connaght's bleak terrain apparently made the choice a hard one.

So the west of Iona was the place of vision and of the spirit. In line with the solitary tradition of the desert monks, proven members of the community were permitted to live apart as hermits. A small valley to the west of the monastic community's enclosure holds the remains of a beehive hut and is called by a name which has been translated "The Hermit's Cell."

Iona functioned symbolically and literally as "Tir Na N'Og," the Land of the Dead and of Eternal Life. It is thought that the pre-Christian folk brought their dead there to be buried in the deathless land, securing for them a good place in the Other World. Bodies were brought ashore at Martyr's Bay and there placed on a small hillock, the site of which is still remembered on maps as the "Hill of the Dead." Then, after feasting, the body would be born along the Street of the Dead and buried at or near the present Reilig Odhrain. Later, candidates for the monastery landing at Martyr's Bay would accomplish by their landing a symbolic death and resurrection into their new life as monks. No wonder I was so moved on the beach.

Bob warned us of clambering about the rugged terrain alone. I smiled, knowing I was coming back to Cnoc Mor by myself.

At dinner, a spectacular sight — a double rainbow, perfect arches that glowed, the most vivid of which framed Fionnphort across the sound. I stood with Bob and Kelly as they gazed. I said, "If I were here with my lovely wife and saw such a sight, I would be sure to give her a kiss for luck." They obliged, not suffering over-much as they did.

Just as each tiny stretch of Iona beach, each hill and stone has a name and a meaning and a story, so did each moment, each conversation, each experience on that holy isle become fraught with meaning. At the time I thought, is this only true at sacred places of pilgrimage? Or does pilgrimage serve as a reminder that the whole of our lives, every moment, is fraught with meaning and significance, God speaking, Spirit moving, Christ manifesting, our hearts drawn and enkindled and touched and moved? Only we don't see it, we don't feel it, we forget that all ground is holy and that God is here and that there really is nothing secular or profane except in the boredom and blindness of our minds. Pilgrimage is meant to awaken wonder in the daily, in the sacred path we each are given.

There were moments on Iona when expectation and longing and grace and insight and transformation all came to a nexus, and all I could do was stay still and catch my breath for the wonder of it all.

There was the morning on Cnoc Mor.

I arose early and put my Iona prayer book, small bible, and journal into the patient brown backpack. I left the hotel and walked the empty lanes to the edge of the village. I gazed up, over the fence and the brushy growths along the lane, up the height of Cnoc Mor. I remembered Bob's warning about clambering about alone. The rocks are surprisingly steep and often wet and covered with slick moss and low growth. I did not fear getting hurt so much as I didn't want to scrabble and stumble and make an utter ass of myself. I shrugged, crossed the little ditch and cut through the higher grass to the foot of the hill. I looked up. Naturally terraced with small plateaus and a semblance of natural paths from one to another, often a terrace will not afford access to the next level up but instead leave you at a dead end.

Now, I could have made this up, but I didn't. A large brown rabbit, a hare I suppose, hopped down and sat straight upright, gazing at me. He turned and hopped up one of the ascending routes.

As I said, on pilgrimage one must be alert to and ready to accept one's guides. I climbed hastily after him.

The way proved to be a kind of switchback up the hill. I always found the hare waiting for me, sitting bolt upright. Always he looked before hopping away. Always I followed, and always I found him at the next place which called for a decision.

We were at the top so suddenly that it startled me. The hare sat waiting. I could almost but not quite swear it winked as it turned and, with a flash of white tail, hopped down out of sight on the far side of Cnoc Mor.

I sat on the edge of the rough stone circle on Cnoc Mor's crest and gazed about in wonder. The lightening sky was studded with swift clouds, each carved sharply in the center and shredded to wisps on each edge, scudding swiftly while driven by a southwestern wind, a wind from Ireland. Pale sunlight alternated with cloud-shadow and an occasional splatter of rain. All seemed intensely alive and in motion, from the moaning sea ceaselessly embracing and releasing the western shore of the island to the swift sun climbing like a hare itself into the eastern sky.

Here he sat, the old abba, I thought, and here I sit and am content.

I read the Iona Community's prayers for the day; I shielded my books from the worst of the rain. When I was done, I packed up the books and just sat. I gazed across the sound and let the swift sun warm me as much as the clouds would allow it to. And I prayed for a vision for the parish, for a direction, a way to take the welter of half-articulated needs and expectations and talk about "tradition" and "change" and "ministry" and make of it a shape, something to live for and to live by.

And he came, climbing over the rocks, sometimes hoisting himself up by main strength up the north face of Cnoc Mor, choosing the hardest path. His robe could once have been white, but now it was gray and stained with ink from his copying as well as with soil. His forehead was large and was accentuated by the outlandish tonsure, the shaving of the hair from ear to ear, letting it grow Druid-fashion long and wild in back. His eyes burned. But his speech was gentle and courteous.

He sat down next to me without comment, for after all it was his place, his desert. We talked.

We talked about how hard it is to keep a community on track, and how just when you're ready to give up something new happens — new energy, new grace. I asked him if monks were as stubborn as Episcopalians, and he told me I didn't know the half of it.

I asked him for a vision for the parish, for Saints Peter and Paul. He said that the vision had been granted, but that we'd have to work for it, to name it as well as to live it. I said something sarcastic, whereupon he said, "You wouldn't want it to be cheap, now," as he playfully took a swipe at my head.

The sun climbed higher and shone bright. He was gone, faded like the drying dampness on the heather or, like the hare, perhaps he hopped back down from stone to stone. I don't know which. I arose stiff, and definitely did not hop like a hare as I slowly descended the east side path.

All I know of visions is that they are born some place between the eyes, deep in, at a place where the eyes and the brain descend into the heart. I don't think they are heard with the ears or seen with the eyeballs. I tell you this, not to recount some tale of wonder or demonstrate my need for anti-hallucinatory drugs, but to tell you plainly how it is I remember. It's the only way I know to tell the tale.

chapter 13

the thin place

G EORGE MacLEOD, famed strong-willed Church of Scotland cleric and twentieth-century Celtic visionary, is credited with calling Iona a "thin place," a place that welcomes seekers but, he assures, only as pilgrims seek "shall they truly find." Lord George himself sought to recapture the wild, lusty soul of the ancient Celtic Christian faith, a faith he wished to live out not just on Iona's peaceful, isolated rock but in the desperate inner city. He recruited a mixed group of soft-handed clergy and hard-bitten laborers and craftsman to journey to Iona with stone and mortar. They lived together while they rebuilt the ruined Benedictine monastery. Contemporaries commented wryly on the comic mismatch of the bookish clerics and the crusty workers, and how iron-lunged MacLeod would roust them from bed at dawn and have them all plunge into the icy waters of the sound. Perhaps the real miracle of Iona is that they didn't flay Lord George alive on the spot and use *his* blood to firm the mortar, making him a member of the Oran club. Blood was apparently not necessary as a building adhesive. But Lord George found the gutsy faith he sought.

I sought this faith, and found it. I found other surprising things.

Bob and Kelly Wilhelm led us early one day down the southeast coast of the little island, telling some tales of the houses along the way. A small cottage at a crossroads is named Tigh Shee. The maps translate this as "House of Peace," but this is either prevarication or reticence to speak its true name aloud. "House of the Fairies" it is literally, and Bob said the locals know that if you live there that there are certain doors you leave open and certain passageways you do not block. For Tigh Shee is built on a fairy road, and so long as the Fair Folk can continue to pass

71

along it unseen yet unimpeded then all is well. One does not wish to be nearby if all is not well.

The group broke up after a leisurely walk and I stood alone at the edge of a tiny beach. I let the small rhythmic waves wash over my soul and I drank almost greedily of the peace. It seemed like so long since I had had any real peace that lasted longer than two minutes. To my left I heard music like bells. I walked toward the foot of a small cliff and found a path. It led to a tiny copse where water was welling from the cliff face and falling to rocks below.

I felt sure I was in an enchanted place. I pulled a white handkerchief from my pocket — fortunately unused — and tore a small strip from the edge which I tied to the thorny, red-berried sapling growing by the freshet's side. I took off my cap and prayed I would be allowed to return to that place one day.

From there I walked slowly up a rising glen, green and silent, surrounded by natural stone walls. After a few minutes of drinking in the silence the unmistakable sense that I was not alone stole over me. It was a fairy place, I was and am sure, and the Good Folk thronged around unseen. I smiled although I trembled slightly from the uncanny sense of it all, and thanked the Fair Folk, friends of my ancestors, for allowing me to come home for a visit. I hope they thought that I was polite.

Bob and Kelly took us north one day to the Hill of the Seat, the traditional site where monks and penitents would serve ordeals, likely "cross-figil" with arms stretched out wide. "A vision or a blow" was the vow taken there, said Bob. Paul, one of the therapists from St. Louis, climbed to the top of the beetling rock and braved the wind to stand with his arms outstretched.

Later I came back alone, tired after a fretful, empty-feeling afternoon. When I climbed to the top of the harsh, keen-edged rock and stood, I found myself praying to be freed of fear and of self-hatred and of foolish worry.

The keen wind cleansed me and left me lighter. A small boat braved the choppy seas to the east as some black-clad figure danced with abandon on the smooth grass to the north. I don't know if the dancer was some free-spirited young European, a fairy out of the *tuath* for the day, or a vision of some addled monk of a millennium ago, enjoying a turn on the grass out of stern Columba's eyes. On Iona, the answers to such questions just do not seem very relevant.

I walked from there over the fields to the lugubrious stretch of beach to the northeast: the White Strand of the Monks.

I have Danish blood on my father's side, and starting with a love of Vikings as a kid I have never lost interest in the Norse part of my heritage. To this day I can tell tales of the Norse gods and goddesses, and I even know the names of the runes, the ancient carved figures that bore meaning and sound and magic all at once.

As I stood on that tiny beach which still seems to mourn the monks butchered by the Norse in that first Viking raid, I felt the confusion and the sadness and the irony of history and the passing of the centuries. There I stood on the beach where my kin slew my kin and voices cried to Christ while voices roared of Odin and the "blood-eagle" was carved by axes on monkish backs. I stooped and ran my hands through the sand. They came away damp, as if the sands were still steeped in blood.

With the old cane I was using as a walking-staff I slowly traced a Thor's Hammer upon the sands, shuddering as I made the pagan sign, the despoiler's sign, on the holy isle. I stood back and gazed. Then I reached forth the cane again and slowly drew a circle about the hammer, adding another vertical bar to its underside to make it a Celtic cross. Under the cross I wrote "Pax" in Latin script and again in Norse runes. And I prayed — for the long-dead monks, for reconciliation, for an end to greed and violence, for all innocent victims of exploitation and war. I thrust the cane into the sand next to the sigil and took a picture which I still have. The cane looks like a shepherd's staff.

The white sand was cold and still save for the barest whisper of breeze which turned it over grain by grain. The sea-birds were silent. I thought of all the war dead of the ages, all those dead at the hands of the violent and the greedy. They crowded onto that strip of lonely beach, assembled in silence. I raised my frail hand in silent blessing over them all and slowly, heavily walked away.

The rest of my time on Iona comes to me with no sense of sequence. There were vivid moments of focused experience, interspersed with times of emptiness and waiting. These were often lonely and fraught with a sense of gloom and isolation. My shield against this was prayer and reminding myself that I was here on pilgrimage. I strove to make friends with my down times, and remembered that Philip Cousineau spoke of the "brooding" that comes over one on pilgrimage. So I would pray, in silence, using no or very simple words. I would find a quiet and un-remarkable place, a bench or an out-of-the-way soft chair, or my small room with its hot pot ready to make the ubiquitous tea. I would write and sketch. At such times I would become aware of something coming to birth slowly in me, in darkness and silence.

These were rich if perplexing times. Other times were just kind of hard, when I would miss my family and just want to cuddle into our tiny, noisy, messy, wonderful house back home with all its young bursting life. I missed my wife with an enveloping mix of loneliness and desire and an odd sense of being incomplete. Our anniversary came and went, and I missed her like a fire in my flesh, my fiery wife with whom I can fight as fiercely as I can love. I briefly felt like I was at war, missing her as I was stuck at the "front."

Sometimes the romantic blinders would drop from my eyes, and I stopped peering through the mists to see long-dead saints and heroes and would see with clarity the local people, here and now, who struggle to squeeze a living from Iona's stony soil and cold, tumultuous sea, and from the endless sea of tourists as well. The shopkeepers, trying to make one last round of sales before the weather closed and most of the hotels and B&B's closed with it and the long, lean winter set in. The college-aged girl, pierced, overweight, and somewhat sullen, who told me she worked here summers for school money and who clearly intended to be anywhere but Iona as soon as she could afford it. Life is hard in the Hebrides, as an articulate young political activist told our group. Since the trauma of the Highland Clearances which followed the final defeat of Scotland's armed forces by the British, the island way of life has never fully recovered. Life in the islands is misunderstood by virtually every outsider who comes there either to pillage or to impose well-intentioned philanthropy.

On Wednesday I walked the pilgrimage led by the Iona Community from Tor Abb at the monastery, to Columba's Bay in the south, to Dun I in the north.

It was driving rain. The wind made the rainfall more horizontal than vertical. The dedicated Iona Community people, sanely clad in boots and waterproof everything, led us on a winding way through the fields to the southern toe of the island. It was the mix of people, the spectacle of pilgrims gathered from many lands and walking together, that moved me. A vital Australian couple, friendly and warm, much better than I at remembering names, who greeted me next day on a footpath with a cheery, "All right then, Kurt?" A Dutch evangelical pastor, spare of frame with a modest balding head, who marched gamely over the slick rocks and the dripping heather singing deep guttural Dutch hymns, fit for a marching sort of Christianity from another time and place. A nice upper-middle class Yank lady who told me of her cancer and the journey that she undertook at mid-life that led to Iona. An octogenarian lady in cloth coat and babushka, who flew in the face of the admonishments of the Iona Community staff to wear boots and slipped along in flat shoes with nylon stockings. We helped her, carried her at need.

The end of the island — driving rain, ancient cairns of piled stones left by centuries of pilgrims, a beach of pebbles facing invisible Ireland. There stands the "cairn of the back to Ireland," where legend says Columba stood and peered toward distant Ulster, making sure that he was complying with his penance and that his newfound desert was truly out of sight of his beloved land. Then he turned and, shedding tears of grief, slowly and heavily went about the business of making his monastic home. The tears are there — lovely stones of a translucent green, "Columba's tears," which the sharp-eyed can collect among the riot of rocks. I found two. The best my wife has to this day, my own tear shed as I thought upon her.

The other story of the stones is that they were the tears of a mermaid shed upon falling in love with one of Columba's monks. She learned to her and the young monk's sorrow of the dim view Columba took of one of his monks renouncing celibacy and beginning a "ménage a mer" with her. I think her daddy the Sea King was not thrilled with the match either. I held the green stone tears and grinned in the rain, shaking my head for all the reasons our hearts may be broken. One tear for Columba, one for the unnamed mermaid — I like both stories, so on that beach they both can be true.

I felt wetter than any time I had ever gone swimming or taken a shower. My clothes were twice their normal weight, my shoes were sponges. Water, water everywhere, not a potty in sight — I bitterly regretted the last cup of tea I drank that morning.

Trucks awaited us on the Machair, the plain which was the farmland of the ancient community. Water, hot chocolate, and tea — welcome but a warm port-a-john would have been even more refreshing. There at last the Iona Community folk called the game on account of rain, assuring us that we were stalwart and brave, a match for any pilgrims of yore.

I trudged along the road home, through the Vespers Gate, the path that the monks would take when the monastery bell would call them from field work to the evening Office. My sodden brain had the stubborn thought that since I may never return I was going to finish the pilgrimage on my own feet, by God and Columba's butt. A bus pulled up, the young woman driving peering incredulously at me. In a thick working-class British accent, she muttered, "Need a lift?"

I preferred to finish walking, I retorted.

She scowled. "Oh, get in, then," she said in disgust.

Secretly glad to be ordered into self-preservation, I climbed in and the bus, crammed with silent, marinated humanity, snarled its way back to the village.

I burst into a dry and cozy parlor, lit by a peat fire, where Bob and Kelly and the rest of the seminar group were hearing of great deeds rather than doing them in the wild and the wet. I dripped and must have glared, for their eyes widened in alarm. Bob intoned, "And the young one stood in the door, wild-eyed."

"If anyone needs me, I'll be getting wet again, in the bath. And don't look for the Scotch bottle," I announced.

I took the bottle of single-malt that the Franciscan had thoughtfully left in our meeting room. I lowered myself into a hot bath and put a respectable dent in the bottle. I felt much drier as I did so.

The tiny library building of Iona hosts a fine cultural program. That night the guest was a lovely Scots singer who sang songs, some traditional, some of her own composition, in Gaelic. Between songs, she spoke of the pain and exile of the "Wild Geese," the Celtic people who fled into exile to the Americas and to Australia in order to find safety from the British and to make a new life. Poignantly, the "Wild Goose" is used today by some Celtic-inspired Christians, chiefly the Iona Community, to signify the Holy Spirit.

My shoes were still sodden masses twice their normal weight, but I tried to ignore the squish as I closed my eyes and let the woman's songs sweep me away. Wild winds, cries of battle and of pain, monk's chants and rich robes seen through a haze of smoke. Receding coasts, terrible hunger in the gut and hunger in the heart.

Outside, the stars blazed with a light I had never seen. The Milky Way lay stretched out like a road of cream. I thought suddenly of Santiago, the "Strange Road" in northern Spain leading to the shrine of St. James near the Atlantic coast, the medieval pilgrim road that one can still walk.

The next day, I met again my fellow American pilgrim, Joanie from Seattle. She told me of her own pilgrim way on the island. She said it was time for her to leave, and wondered where she should go next.

The creamy band of stars of the night before leaped to my mind. "To Santiago," I blurted out. "The Strange Road, the Milky Way, the road to Santiago."

She looked at me in wonder. "Yes. Thank you. Yes. Santiago was on my mind when I got up this morning. I'm leaving today. Santiago is next."

We never know when we serve as signposts to other pilgrims. We are meant to offer and to accept help and guidance both. It's true on Iona, and it's true everywhere.

Then there were the fairies, and the way of the fay.

Next day I walked with the seminar group partway to Columba's Bay, along the old pilgrim trail. Bob stopped next to Cnoc an Tobair, the

Hill of the Spring within which reign the Fairy Folk as Bob recounted. An actual spring wells from one side. The top was thick with ravens. Bob spoke of the ancient stories of the hollow hills and the Sidhe, the fairy folk who live within them, in a world enchanted with *glamour*, their lovely but deceptive magic. I shuddered slightly as I watched the mob of ravens on the fairy hill.

We walked further along the road to the Hill of the Angels. This is where, according to legend, a monk spying on Columba in his solitude saw him at prayer surrounded by a host of angels. Like so many Celtic Christian stories, this one is set at a place that was apparently sacred before the Christian time. Within memory the islanders would ride horses clockwise round and round the foot of the Hill of the Angels on St. Michael's Day. The practice may have descended from a rite of praise and sacrifice to the sun god. So heaven meets earth there, pagan meets Christian, and Columba found the angels just as did Jacob at Beth El, the House of God, at the borders of Canaan.

The group went on, and I left them to walk slowly back to the fairy-haunted hill and crossroads.

I tell this tale with hesitation, as the more practical reader may have already dismissed me as a romantic lunatic. But I was raised to tell a tale as a tale and so be courteous to the folk who share our world through stories and dreams. Sometimes the veil of disbelief and the everyday parts briefly, and we and those on the other side blink at one another in surprise. Perhaps they are as startled as we.

Ahead on the otherwise deserted road loomed a large black form. I stared, the faint metal taste of fear in my mouth. It looked a huge black dog, impossibly thin and large. It sat, gazing up the road at me.

Feeling that I had no choice but to go on, I did so. The black presence waited. Then it moved toward me. As it did so, it became the shape of a woman. Tall, very tall, and almost impossibly thin, with long straight hair and a long, pale, elliptical face. Dressed in black she was, something between a cloak and a coat. She kept to her side of the road, and I to mine.

I smiled as we slowly passed one another. I touched my forehead and said, "Good day."

She smiled then, her face becoming inexpressibly sweet. She nodded her head and, in a low, thrilling voice, said, "Good day to you."

Something in me melted with gratitude. The fairy folk are in the blood and the soul of anyone whose roots are Celtic. I felt they had welcomed me, and tears came to my eyes as enchantment still lives and walks our earth. Today there is precious little room for wonder, and for magic, and for hope.

All the same, the Way of the Fay, their illusory magic, is said to be that of shadows and *glamour* that fades under scrutiny. I thought of the role that anxiety and irrational fear had played in my life, keeping me from taking risks, from living with abandon, my personal "Way of the Fay."

At the crossroads, I turned. She was gone, nowhere to be seen.

The house at the crossroads was the home of a retired stonemason. As I examined the stones for sale on which he had carved crosses, he emerged and blessed me with stories.

He told me how Columba was an aristocrat and came to the island with a royal retinue. He told me that the legends of Columba casting out local priests who opposed him did not refer to Druids, but to Christian monks of the Ninian/Kentigern tradition. He spoke of ley lines, invisible currents of earth-energy in which many believe and along which one will find many a holy place, Christian and otherwise. He claimed that Iona is "uncanny" because on the island several of these ley lines intersect. And he told me of an ancient stone circle, pre-Christian and relatively unnoticed, and how to find it.

I found it on my last full day.

It lies very close to the *vallum*, the ancient Christian monastic enclosure wall, on the east coast of the island slightly more than halfway north. Its eastern edge is partly submerged. The ground there lies low and is swampy.

The stones are low, and unless you are seeking the circle they seem only a collection of boulders. If you look closely, though, you see that the circle is perfect, with a central stone, one to the side that is altar-like, and a stone outside the circle that to me suggested a stone of preparation for ritual.

I stood in the chill sunlight, within sight of a modern house and farm, outside the circle. Silently I invoked the Holy Trinity and their encircling protection, then I greeted any of the Old Ones who were still present. I announced my presence to them, as a descendant come from far to touch home soil again and to pay his respects.

I touched the preparation stone and thought of vessels, bowls, cups, and knives. I shuddered and moved into the circle.

As I passed one stone, I saw on its side a sigil freshly painted that I did not understand but that suggested an astrological sign. Cursing under my breath at the foolish meddler who had tried to invoke the power of the circle and its slumbering spirits, I walked warily on.

The altar stone seemed to shimmer with dark power, dangerous. I raised my hand and, tracing the cross, gave it a wide berth.

I stood in the center and straightened my spine, breathed. I could still see the house and its satellite dish, but it was remote, an image from another time. I stood in the circle's time, another, an older time.

I spoke aloud and thanked God and the saints for bringing me there. Then I drew a long breath and thanked the Old Ones, the people and the heroes and yes, the old spirits, who had given song and poetry and legends and visions and laws to my ancient ancestors. I told them I was glad there were still places where they could be found. I told them I hoped they could dwell here undisturbed.

I left the circle. As I walked through the sodden growth, I was startled three times, my heart beating wildly. Three times the ground in front of me erupted as a grouse leaped skyward, wings whirring.

I grinned shakily and thanked the Old Ones for having a sense of humor, and for giving me a sign using the sacred Three, hard on the heart rate though it was.

An old Gaelic prayer directed to God yet referring to the fairy folk begins, "We accept their protection yet reject their leading...." It is a courteous way to live, acknowledging that we inhabit neither the earth nor the spirit world alone. It is rude to not acknowledge, and arrogant too, but it is humility to acknowledge our limits as well. The community of which we are a part is vast beyond our imagining. We have our boundaries, and they have theirs.

I was to leave Iona the next day. I had been incredibly gifted, and yet was leaving behind so much, so much I hadn't seen and done. I had not lived with the Iona Community, I had not climbed Din I and bathed in the Spring of Youth. I had not walked the full borders of the island, had not prayed in the hermit's glen, the Cell of the Culdee. But greed is unbecoming in a pilgrim, spiritual greed most of all. Fearful yet full, I prepared to depart.

chapter 14

fear and flight

I HAD NO CLEAR PLAN after leaving Iona. Iona had been a cozy nest, with built-in support and friendship from the group members. I remembered my old brave days (or were they naive?) in the Philippines, when I would head into the back country with a shoulder bag and a few pesos and a vague general destination. Now I was middle-aged and anxious. As we checked out, the group was already tangibly dissolving, each couple filled with a sense of their next destination, confident in their previous travels together. The only other solo pilgrim, the Franciscan with Scottish roots, knew where he was bound — Oban for a couple days' stay in some hotel that he described as pricey but beautiful and restful. All seemed content but me.

I tried to contain my fretting but I think it showed. I roamed the ferry decks and felt a ghost of the old anxiety that had been a galling souvenir of Southeast Asia. I smiled at the appearance of an old acquaintance that, like it or not, is part of me.

Once in Oban, I boarded the Glasgow train. I learned that the train connection straight from Oban to Stranraer in Ireland would involve a transfer between those two awkward train stations in Glasgow. So it began to look like an unexpected extra night in Glasgow for me.

It was Friday afternoon in Glasgow when we arrived, and the hustle of street traffic disoriented me. I took off with my luggage to find the other train station and got utterly, completely lost. I walked down some very upscale-looking pedestrian mall streets, with the locals glancing curiously at the harried-looking outsider with tattered tweed coat and dragging luggage. Hopelessly lost, I stood and blinked.

A kindly looking woman walked straight up to me. She was dressed in dark clothes, with a face that was neither young nor old, beautiful nor homely. In a musical Scottish accent, she asked if I was "turned around a bit" and was I a tourist? "A pilgrim," I said, and her eyes misted. She asked if I had seen "our Iona" and "our Cathedral." I had indeed, I said, whereupon she took my arm and asked where I needed to go. Hoping that she did not want to lead me somewhere private to negotiate a different sort of pilgrim experience, I decided that anywhere was better than standing on that yuppie Scottish mall, and accepted.

As we walked the woman, who never told me her name, said she was a member of the Cathedral chapter. I told her of finding St. Kentigern in the crypt. "Lower cathedral," she insisted, "we call it the lower cathedral." She said she was delighted that pilgrims were coming to the old holy places in increasing numbers.

I looked up and we were standing outside the doors of a busy railroad station. "Here then you are," she announced. She took my face in her two hands and kissed me on the lips. "Come back again," she smiled, and turned and disappeared into the crowd.

The date was September 29, feast of Michael the Archangel. Was she the most affectionate and kindly eccentric member of Glasgow Cathedral Chapter? Or was she Brigid, in wise matron-crone guise? Or maybe Michael himself in drag?

Pilgrims need to be cunning as foxes, yet innocent as doves. There is a long tradition of pilgrims getting fleeced by con artists. There's an equally long tradition of pilgrims being helped by angels.

I learned that there was one train ticket that you could buy that would take you to Stranraer, then by ferry to Belfast, but that the next such train would leave next morning.

I walked and walked, and fetched up at a humble B&B which taught me a valuable lesson: that I am neither as flexible nor as democratic as I thought I was. Dark and run down, my room depressed me with its stained sheets and used-Pamper-colored walls. After some of my fellow guests rolled in drunk and shouting various "fooks" and "shites," and after I saw the proprietor turn away an Asian-appearing family even though I knew he had empty rooms, I bailed. Leaving him the eighteen pounds, I found my way back to my more comfortable if more pricey Theatre Hotel. Some prayer, a soft bed, and a call home left me in a much more philosophical frame of mind.

But not before the nearly blind led the blind.

I had pushed out into the night to find some perfectly dreadful food, and was trying to walk off both the gravy and my desolation. On a dark and lonely street I met someone even more harried than I. His shoulders hunched as he dragged a heavy valise. Exhaustion and anxiety fought for space on his face with his look of stolid courage. I recognized him as my singing Dutch pastor from the pilgrim walk on Iona.

He seemed at the end of his rope, even more turned around by Glasgow's narrow labyrinth of streets than had been I. I asked him if he needed a place to stay, but all he could repeat was that he wanted to find the train station "and sleep there, so I can get my train first thing in the morning." Knowing more than my Dutch friend at least, I pointed the way. He had a long way to walk.

On the Feast of Michael, you never know when you may be called upon to be Michael, and help another pilgrim even amidst your own fears.

I slept, five hours only but deeply, and woke refreshed next day. But I was ready to quit Glasgow and continue my journey. My heart and soul were already half in Ireland.

chapter 15

"I'll show you around a bit"

NEXT MORNING, the dingier parts of Glasgow slipped past the train windows, and the rather desperate-looking urban landscape gave way gradually to exurbs, then to countryside. The lovely Lowlands caressed the windows. We passed small town after small town, with locals boarding and de-training. Finally the train pulled into a desolate collection of tracks besides a huge awning. Grabbing my bags and following the throng, I found myself in a huge anteroom: the ferry waiting area. More airport lobby than bus station, with TVs blaring and seats holding bored-looking, sleepy travelers.

A boarding call, then a most thorough luggage search coupled with a metal detector allowed me to mount the steps to the ferry. A huge, cavernous ark of a ship, its belly was filling with cars and huge semi trucks as rapidly as its decks were filling with people.

I wandered the decks, replete with shops, a theater, restaurants, and pubs, plural. Watching folks cozying up to pints while casually watching the big ship pull away from its pier, I bitterly regretted the Dramamine I'd taken anticipating rough autumn seas. The ferry was subject to the barest of perceptible rolls on its whole voyage. I regretted as well my distrustful decision to not check my bags, eliciting glances of mild pity from fellow travelers as I grunted my way through the passenger decks.

Sitting in comfy chairs, one for me and one for bags, I relaxed a bit and contrasted my travel fretting with the comfort of the voyage. I chatted mentally with Columba, whose voyage to Iona I was reversing across the Irish Sea. It was harder going in a skin coracle versus the ferry's easy luxury. I am not the man you were, Columba, I told him silently. But I felt my exile nonetheless.

A clown worked the deck, making balloon animals for kids and pretty women. He stopped for quite some time near me, for several seats down were a pretty young mom and child. The young mom was lovely. The little girl was adorable, blond, and curious and active, roaming the deck and charming people. The pair made me ache for my children and for my wife, parenthood and loneliness and *eros* all intertwined and leaving me feeling like a gaping hole in the road. I had an impulse to chat them up, but resisted as I distrusted my motives and suspected I wanted to flirt, however innocently. The impulse felt wrong — I am a pilgrim, I thought, and married as well, so if I am meant to feel lonely and horny and empty then I shall feel that. Besides, images of being beaten by some jealous British soldier-husband flitted across my mental screen, and so the mom and little girl continued their journey unaware that they had been spared the attentions of a lonely middle-aged American husband and dad.

In about the time that it would have taken Columba to say Mass, the ferry docked at Belfast.

I was met at the gate by William, nephew-in-law of one of my parish members, a strong-looking graying man casually dressed in jeans and a waterproof jacket. After all the boarding and arriving done in solitude, it felt good and healing to be met by someone who knew my name and was expecting me.

William boosted my gear into the boot of his car, and we forged ahead into the traffic of Belfast. "Since you're not here for long," he said casually, "I'll show you around a bit."

With that said, he took me down the Falls Road.

I tensed when I realized where we were. Growing up in the '70s, I was almost as aware of the Irish "Troubles" of that time as I was of the Vietnam War. Names like Christchurch, Londonderry, and Bobby Sands loomed large and ominous. But chief among them was the Falls Road, flashpoint for riots and for bombs and for death.

I was prepared for a tense and devastated area. I was unprepared for the teeming, bustling life I saw. Everywhere there were people and well-kept buildings. But there were hints nevertheless. A headquarters of the Catholic faction, all green and gold and tricolor Irish Republican flags. There were murals of the same theme — beautiful artistic quality, art in the service of civil war. Then, a turn and about-face, and our car coasted through the Protestant-Unionist neighborhood — all red, blue, and white, even the curbs painted so, British flags everywhere, and a feeling of watchful tension. And the murals — like the Catholic ones, evoking God and the Trinity and Christ and the heroes of ancient Ireland and the blood of the martyred fighters. One only had to change a few words and a few choices of color: the bloodthirsty, intractable message was the same.

I asked how things now stood and William allowed as how they were quieter. "Most of us just want peace." He told of his job as an air traffic controller in the '70s, newly married, and his wife, Denise, working downtown. The news would come of another bomb and those who had family in the affected area were released to go seek them. William would drive his car as far as possible until coming up against the inevitable British Army checkpoint sealing off the downtown area. Then he'd get out and the search on foot began. "I'd look all day to see if my wife was alive. And that's how we lived in those days."

He brought me to their lovely, comfortable home and I spent a few days in the heart of a warm Irish family.

William and Denise were in the end process of shipping off their eldest boy, John, to college in London. I sat in the comfortable parlor with William sipping a glass of Irish whiskey as he told of the ferry journey with "his things." We sat in silence. I thought of my own boy, and how the irony of parenting meant that if we had loved him and did our job decently then he too would feel empowered to leave our home, break that tie. I crossed the room and clinked glasses with another father. "To our sons," I said.

Next day, Denise took me about. First we picked up her parents, a lovely elderly pair still living in the "old neighborhood." The neat but narrow working-class row house made me think of the stories I'd heard of the British Army pulling down the staircases of suspect houses. The one staircase in the central hall of these houses is suspended and vulnerable. The practice is a mean, effective way to leave a message of compliance.

Denise brought us to a monastic ruin — Inch Abbey, a French Cistercian foundation of the local Norman overlord John de Coursey. In a practice all too familiar in Ireland and Scotland, the invader ousted an older Celtic monastic community to establish his own "foreign" monks, church and crown at work together. I glanced around the site to see if I could detect any trace of the older Celtic community — remnants of the *vallum*, the surrounding earthen wall, or even the base of a stone high cross. But a cursory glance revealed nothing. Only an archaeologist with patience could find such remnants as might remain, and for a second I silently cursed the Celtic monastic custom of building lightly with earth and wattle and daub, leaving it to the Continental monks to build with more durable Gothic stone.

But still, Inch Abbey is part of Ireland's monastic heritage, and the pattern of the ruined buildings was classically Benedictine and felt instantly familiar to me. Despite the heavy rain, I prowled the ruins with Denise, knelt and prayed at what was obviously the remnants of the high altar footing, and felt the presence of the Benedictine community once there. For all my prattling about Celts, there is a Benedictine part of my soul as well — I co-founded a clergy group covenanted to an adaptation of the Benedictine Rule, and when younger was so taken by the romanticism of Thomas Merton's writings that I imagined myself a Benedictine or Cistercian monk. The more realistic and rather disillusioned writings of the "later Merton" accompanied my dawning disillusionment with any structure that one hopes will solve one's own spiritual conflict and struggle — I once thought that the right monastery or community would resolve my doubt and issues and struggle with God and self and others. Now I do not expect any such order or structure or denomination or congregation or vocation to do this for me. It's enough to have a community in which it is safe to ask and wrestle with real questions and doubts and loves. That is more than many ever find.

All of this tumbled about in my soul as I roamed and touched and knelt at Inch Abbey, sometimes seeing out of the corner of my eye the wisp of the white and black-clad brethren passing by at their many tasks.

Denise trailed after me, no doubt thinking me mad but saying that she was amazed to be learning things about a ruin in her own town, one that she visited for picnics, from a foreigner who had never seen the place.

We all must see our homes through the eyes of a pilgrim. Perhaps only in this way may we get to know the place for the first time.

From Inch Abbey Denise drove us to Downpatrick, site of a large Anglican cathedral and one of the primary sites connected with St. Patrick. Some medieval records claim that Patrick was buried here along with Brigid, and that Patrick and Brigid's tombs, set side-by-side, were found to have moved apart to make room for Columba between them when his body was brought from Iona for re-burial. All this is a matter of legend now, since no remnants of any Celtic-era tombs have been positively found. The great church claims to be built over Patrick's bones with no evidence to substantiate the claim. But that does not matter once one is inside.

Frankly I disliked the interior of the church. For me it embodied the worst of empire-era Anglicanism. The arrangement of pews, boxes, and stalls for the chapter spoke eloquently of caste distinction, and the officiant's desk facing the bishop's throne doubled, as the signage said, as a judge's seat. Crown and cross, scepter and crosier, God and nation — Constantine's church, a relic at Downpatrick but alive and well in other parts of the world.

As much as I disliked the church interior, there was a presence.

It was silent, a tomblike silence, deep and beyond life and even death. It was strong, and without fanfare or words it welcomed me. I knelt at the altar rail and placed my hand on the flagstones of the floor. They were cold, yet vibrant. Tomb or not, Patrick was there.

I knelt in silence and spread open on the stones the pilgrim journal of prayers. Sudden understanding, either Patrick's understanding or understanding Patrick, washed over me. Patrick understood exile, he understood loneliness. And he understood courage. I stayed in place and let him tell me silently of courage.

I stood and gathered the journal. I walked out into the day struggling with light and shadow and rain, and Patrick's courage came with me.

I've always loved a good cemetery, and a good Irish cemetery — well, there's nothing not to like. I walked happily with Denise among the streaming stones.

A large boulder stands in the midst of Downpatrick's cemetery. On its top is carved a lovely whorled Celtic cross with "Padraic" carved in Celtic uncial style. Shrugging at the knowledge that some wealthy Irish romantic placed the stone here in the nineteenth century, having no idea where Patrick's actual dust lay, I knelt and kissed the stone, prayed. A slightly disheveled-looking man, smoking a cigarette stub and with an embarrassed-looking woman in tow, spotted me and strolled over. He stood next to me in a companionable way, gazing down at the stone with me. The distinct smell of beer and tobacco reminded me of Ireland too, Ireland as embodied in my family members back in New York.

"You on holiday then?"

"Pilgrim."

"Ah, *sha sha*, pilgrim. Here to see Patrick's grave then?"

"Yes."

"Well, they placed the stone there, but he's not buried here, not buried here a'tall. He's in Armagh, where I'm from. If you came with me then, back to Armagh, you'd see where he is then. Downpatrick just put this here to compete with Armagh, don't you know. . . . " He went on, making the case for Armagh, and I stood in the streaming day, liking the conversation and the man and glad that once again the Trickster had come to lighten me the hell up and break up the day.

I politely resisted allowing the man to drive me to Armagh, to Denise and the man's companion's obvious relief.

That night, the whole extended family took me out for an elegant dinner, a country club I think it was. It was a joy and delight, just eating and talking and laughing and looking at all the pretty Irish faces and hearing the soft music of the Irish speech. Two lovely teenage girls pulled up chairs and plied me with questions; Denise later told me they only really wanted to hear my "cute accent." But the greatest treat of the night came with Denise's old dada sitting opposite me. I had grown up with a number of Irish maxims, so as we rose to go I looked him in the eye and clutched my worn black cap. Shaking it, I said, "I had a hat when I came in...."

He smiled, a twinkle in his eye, "And you'll have a hat when you go out."

My old Grandpa Ed was famous for that line. He was famous for the brawls it provoked as well. Dead these forty-seven years, I know he smiled.

Next day, Denise raced through intersections and roundabouts to put me on the Dublin train. Consciously drawing on a little of Patrick's courage, I boarded the train that crossed the Irish countryside and headed for fabled Dublin.

chapter 16

the monastic city

THE TRAIN TRIP SOUTH was disconcerting. The Irish faces were at once familiar yet strange. The Irish brogues were comforting and comfortable, if not as musical to my ears as the Scottish burrs of Glasgow and Iona, but I felt a stranger as I searched for a seat and a place to stow my gear. All my life long I had lived with a kind of *Quiet Man* romanticism, that being in the Republic of Ireland would be a kind of homecoming. Sitting on the Dublin train, slightly ill at ease, looking at modern Ireland seated around me chatting and reading and commuting, I realized that I was a foreigner. I was a Yank, and although half of my ancestral roots were here, my people had left a century before. They had left a different Ireland, stone-cold poor and hungry and hopeless and desperate and unquestionably, uneasily under the thumb of mother England. The world had seen two world wars and numerous traumas and changes, and Ireland herself had lived through the Easter Uprising of 1916 and the Irish Republic and the Troubles of the 1970s and had moved from being considered a Third World nation to the economic Celtic Tiger of today. Grandpa Patrick and Grandma Bridie and the rest would not have fled looking for work and hope. They would have just re-trained and moved to Dublin and put down a deposit on a nice apartment. Paths part, and the hunger of body and of soul makes choices that carve pathways in the flesh and souls of our children's children.

My brooding reverie lifted a bit as I watched the countryside flying by. Irish towns, Irish fields, Irish ruins. "That tower," I said excitedly to the yuppie-looking young woman next to me, "is surely Norman. And it's right there!" She smiled fleetingly and dove back into her newspaper, no doubt regretting that there were no other empty seats within sight.

The Dublin train station was bustling and purposeful. I walked out with my stuff and, needing to change some pounds sterling to Irish "punts," found a narrow, crowded, tense but polite bank where exchange was made. I re-entered the train station and followed enough people to find a long queue for a taxi.

The young cabbie was a helpful sort, relieving me of my incipient anxiety of driving on the left in a rental car. "Just take it easy and always signal." He pointed out the characteristic Dublin pattern of "quays," the old streets arranged perpendicularly to the river Liffey. In the alien busyness of Dublin, he was a true pilgrim guide, and one that was most welcome. I tipped him generously as he dropped me at the rental agency.

It took the young rental agent a long time to find my reservation and get the car. Once it arrived curbside, a gray Ford-something I had never seen in the States, I stood and stared at it, clutching my papers and circling it like it was a skittish colt. Clumsily I climbed into the right side and shifted it into busy Dublin traffic.

I had long dreamed of knocking around Dublin, but now that I had the means and the chance to do so I could not wait to flee. Sticking strictly to directions, I left the city and, gaining driving confidence, I bored south into increasingly rural and pretty country. The Wicklow Mountains rose gently ahead, yet another place of legend. But right around then I began to wonder if any part of Ireland and the British Isles was *not* some sort of place of legend!

Laragh, the town close by Glendalough, is tucked in a bend of the road and possesses a cluster of B&Bs and an enticing-looking pub. A terrific mural on the pub's wall — a cluster of disconsolate-looking cartoon Vikings, with large noses and helmets pushed down over their eyes, stand morosely at the foot of a Celtic round tower. Out of the upper window of the tower leans a jolly-looking monk, beaming and clutching a pint glass. "Lovely day for a Guinness," he asserts. I figured I was home again.

I checked into a pleasant B&B and, after a pint and a bite to eat by the roaring fire in the pub, settled in for a sleep. I lay in the bed and examined the anxiety that had flickered across my mind and soul throughout the journey. I thought of the fairy folk on Iona, and wondered if the "Way of the Fay" in my life has been the way of anxiety and fruitless worry. Here I was traveling a fairly safe and kindly country, of which I'd dreamed all my life, and I was allowing anxiety to play with my mind and distract me from its joys. I bid my anxiety a firm good-night and got a good night's sleep.

I awoke slowly and deliciously. For the first time I felt the freedom of being on the loose by myself. From the windows, the soft Irish countryside drew my gaze gently from one muted color to another, mellowed by the deepening autumn. For the first time I felt at home. The gentle Irish brogues of the B&B owners only confirmed this.

One profound mystery was why, when I began each day with a breakfast which made the plate creak with protein and fat and starch and ended the day with black thick beer and starchy "pub grub," that I lost weight in Ireland. Crammed full of this mystery and of breakfast's ponderous provender, I sallied forth for the ancient monastic site of Glendalough.

Michael Rogers and Marcus Losack, in their thorough and elegant book *Glendalough: A Celtic Pilgrimage,* do a magnificent job of describing Glendalough, its history, its spiritual significance, and how one might walk it as a pilgrim today. Having already read their book in the States and walked Glendalough with my mind's eye, I was and was not ready to make my own way. Was not, in that I do not think anyone can plan on what they will or will not "get out of" a holy place. All pilgrim paths are different, and the over-planned pilgrimage often comes up empty. But I referred often to their book, and commend it to you whose imagination may be kindled by it and whose feet may begin to itch to walk the Wicklow Valley in this deeply sacred place.

Glendalough ("Valley of Two Lakes") is the well-preserved site of a large and famous Celtic monastic community that endured until the Reformation. It is sacred to the founder St. Kevin, who longed for solitude and his "desert" yet found himself with the mixed blessing of disciples and the role of abbot of a large, busy community. At first settling near the lower of the two lakes, Kevin acquired a reputation for sanctity and for a gentle way with the natural world that later would turn St. Francis of Assisi into a garden statue. One tale on this theme has Kevin stand-ing still in the traditional Celtic prayer-pose of the "cross-vigil," his arms outstretched. A bird came and nested in one of his hands, so Kevin tact-fully remained all season with his arm outstretched until the bird's eggs hatched and the fledglings left the nest.

My arm aches at the very thought, but the story charms with the distinctly Celtic courtesy shown to the sacred creation.

A second tale has Kevin performing another classical early Celtic spir-itual exercise: standing in the lake up to his chest reciting the Psalms. The ancient name for the lower lake is Lough na Peist, the lake of the *peist* or water beast. Apparently one such peist called the lake home and, as Kevin tried to concentrate on his Psalms, the peist twined itself an-noyingly, perhaps sensually, around his legs and torso. I sympathize with Kevin whenever I try to read my morning prayers and our Chihuahua hops into my lap and begins to do something vile with his tongue and crotch. Strikingly enough, the story says that rather than withering the inappropriate serpent with a curse, Kevin took the beast with him to the upper lake. There Kevin lived as a hermit and meditated in a cave, and with time a classical desert-style community of monks grew there. The ruins of this community are still plainly visible from across the lake. Per-haps that is not all that is there — the upper lake is dark and cold and a local man told me people avoid swimming in it for all the tales of drown-ings, even of those who were expert swimmers. I wonder if water beasts are common in the Celtic lands from Loch Ness to Glendalough. The dark ink-blue waters of the upper lake, shadowed by the low mountain guarding Kevin's last desert, is as likely a place for a peist as I have seen.

Losack and Rogers reflect that Kevin's taking of the beast to the upper lake may be symbolic of Kevin treasuring and owning and bringing with him his inner beast, his "shadow," his sensual self. I like that as an integrative story with a Jungian flavor, but as for me I leave the lake to the peist. There let it lie and coil, and wait for another monk who does not mind its slimy caress. In this, I am not the man my forebears were.

Glendalough today covers many acres, and in the manner of Celtic monastic sites does not consist of one grand, castle-like building. Like Iona's community, the main complex was surrounded by an earthen wall

or *vallum,* which was later equipped with stone gates. Within this wall
were a number of separate buildings, several churches, and perhaps outdoor places of worship. In a number of Celtic sites, worship seems to
have taken place outdoors when possible and the early churches were
perhaps places of private prayer, shrines really, only secondarily places
of congregational worship. One large, simple, and old stone high cross
within the enclosure called St. Kevin's Cross may have been such a *lecht*
or gathering-place for worship. And the enclosure does not contain all
the remnants of Glendalough's holy places. Nor does it contain the natural beauty of the place. More a district than a single site, Glendalough
draws the spiritual pilgrim, the historical enthusiast, and the hikers and
vacationers all, a whole sort of place.

The old pilgrim's road led through the Wicklow Gap, snaking down
through the mountains, a long and hard road worthy of the pilgrim who
wanted to feel the weariness of Christ in his feet. There at the place
where the pilgrim trail, now a road, leads down from the mountains and
intersects the road leading from Laragh past Glendalough, is a small upright stone with two incised Latin crosses. I backtracked the old pilgrims,
parking my little sedan in the perfectly paved car park and walking back
up the road to rejoin the old trail. Thrashing about in the roadside bram-
bles and weeds, I found a small sign and conquered the ramshackle fence
to plunge over the weedy bank in search of the first station — Trinity
Church.

Over the tiny rise and through the weeds, a hidden clearing and a
small, intact ruin emerged. Trinity Church is located at a respectable
distance from the "monastic city," and was probably the first church encountered by journeying pilgrims. Rectangular, simple, austere, as usual
open to the sky, Trinity guards a silence and a mystery in its solitude.

I walked around the top of the stone wall of Trinity, again not a
security wall but simply delimiting the first area of sacred space of the
church. Finding no gate, I shrugged and, tossing my brown backpack
down, I jumped and landed heavily on the smooth green sward. Rising
to my feet and grateful that I had not twisted an ankle, I saw too late
the "stile," the stone steps built into Trinity's wall by which a visitor may
descend "the right way." I remembered Jesus in John's Gospel saying,

"...I am the gate for the sheep. All who came before me are thieves and bandits..." (John 10:7–8). Feeling like a naughty kid and perhaps a thief as well, I stood and prayed that no matter what my journey, I might always come in and out by he who is the Gate.

How simple was the interior, and how moving that the roof was now the sky. I stood and faced what was the tiny sanctuary, the place of the altar. I found traces of the stone altar footing. I knelt there and prayed. In an intact windowsill to the rear I traced with my fingers a lovely incised Celtic cross, equal-armed, a mate to the one found on a stone on Iona called "Columba's Pillow."

Rogers and Losack say in their book that Trinity is a good place to ask oneself, "Why have I come?"

In my journal I responded. "I came to seek healing. To affirm the goodness of who I am — body and soul, Protestant and Catholic, sexual yet some sort of *manaig* or married monk. Celtic, Anglican, Roman, Tlingit, Norse, with a touch of the pagan (to keep, as Herbert O'Driscoll suggests, my Christianity sweet and savory). Priest and husband, father and son.... It really is all one. For Christ has made me one. But... 'enter by the narrow door!'"

Losack and Rogers reflect on the intact ruins of Trinity as symbolic of the ruins of Christendom, the so-called "Constantinian" synthesis of empire and culture and state and Church that has characterized Western Christianity since the fourth century. Notions such as the "Christian nation," church membership synonymous with citizenship, and alliance of the aims of the state with "God's interests" are hallmarks of this dying paradigm.

Many of us, I most certainly, hunger for something fresh and new and challenging and not convenient, not accommodated to the culture of this or any other bygone day. I crave a faith and a community that is grateful for the past and seeks wisdom and inspiration there, but tries to walk with confidence into a future that is life-giving, that celebrates the best of the unfolding world and loves the men and women immersed in its struggles, who do not take refuge in fundamentalism or zealous nationalism or a futile grasping at certitudes but instead walk by faith and in hope. Trinity Church's ruins speak of ancient energy and vision poured forth for the challenges of that time, and challenge us to ask where and how God gives fresh energy and vision today. I thought of my high-peaked wooden church with rusting gutters back in Portland, and my people who struggle between hope and fear for the future of the parish.

One always knows, as my pilgrim friend said on Iona, when to leave a holy place and not try to greedily drink it dry. I thanked Trinity and made my way down an overgrown path, dodging cow pies, in the general direction of the monastic city.

I emerged on the edge of the car park and walked across and around the edge of the interpretive building. There before me lay a scene of ravishing beauty that tore open my soul. Right in front of me was a bright stream ringing merrily over stones. Past the far bank and spread out like a dream was a valley of greens highlighted by touches of the gold and crimson of autumn. At the center, standing still and watchful like an ancient lighthouse, was the round tower of Glendalough surrounded by peeping bits of other, much lower stone buildings. I stood and gasped, tears springing to my eyes, staring until my eyeballs ached at ancient Ireland laid out before me. Sometimes life does live up to our dreams.

I walked back to the entrance of the car park where a local man was disconsolately pushing leaves about with a broom. We both looked up as a bus rumbled up the road — shiny, new, with block letters spelling "GLENDALOUGH" on its marquee. The worker waved it in. "First bus already?" I said. The dogged worker bent again over his broom. "Aye, first suckers of the day."

I was still laughing as I walked into the ancient stone gate. I touched the odd, bottle-shaped incised cross at the entrance as I entered.

One does not go far within the monastery gate before one runs into graves — crowded, often haphazard, ranging in age from seventh-century to Mrs. O'Shaughnessy, buried just last week. Glendalough still functions as a local burying ground. The Celtic sense of sacred space endured even after the monastic community was dissolved during the Reformation. The monastery was a portal to heaven, so to be buried there is to be buried at the doorway to eternity. This works both ways — the sacred ground sanctifies the dead, the dead sanctify the ground. I was taught in my childhood not to tread on graves, so I tried to pick my way gingerly about, but finally I gave up. Not walking over the dead at Glendalough is like trying to avoid pebbles at the beach. Rogers and Losack counsel walking on the graves and in so doing thinking of our oneness with heaven and earth. I found this both comforting and chilling. The Glendalough dead may be buried decently deep, but the green smell of the grounds seemed to carry to my nose the faint aroma of the vitality that springs forth from death. Not a tame place, Glendalough, no matter how many shiny buses filled with "suckers" drive up to its gates.

At the center of the enclosure is an impressive ruin — the Cathedral Church of Saints Peter and Paul. The interior is wide, the floor also paved with graves. The rector of Saints Peter and Paul of Portland, Oregon, stood in the ruins of Saints Peter and Paul of Glendalough and breathed. My wooden church would not leave behind such durable ruins. Looking around the roofless interior, I thought, "They really need a capital funds campaign."

In my mind's eye, the interior filled with monks clad in gray Celtic wool, moving restlessly about the many tasks that made up daily life in the great church.

A tall, very simple high cross, ringed and devoid of apparent ornamental carving, stands in the grounds and is called simply "St. Kevin's Cross." I walked around it, touched and kissed it. Many of the ancient relics of Celtic Christian Ireland assume new mythic life as "wishing places." Kevin's Cross is no exception — the story has it that if you stand with your back to the cross and can touch your hands behind it, you will be granted your wish. I stood and gingerly experimented with just how hard this could be — it's a big thick cross. I walked away, thinking that only the most elastic and determined would find luck reaching behind Kevin's Cross.

The great Round Tower of Glendalough stands hard by the Cathedral ruins. Its conical roof has been repaired, and I watched entranced as croaking ravens flew in and out of its windows. Scholars debate the actual purpose of the round towers, one of the most characteristic relics of Celtic monasticism. The ancient Gaelic name for the towers was *cloigtheach,* which literally means "bell tower." They were never carillons with great hanging bells, but perhaps a hammered sheet-metal hand-held bell was rung from the top window to signal the canonical hours of prayer. In this sense the round towers were more minarets than carillons — symbols of soaring prayer, calling the faithful both by sound as well as by impressive presence.

The doorway to the round tower is high off the ground and must be reached by a narrow, steep walkway or a ladder. Some speculate that the towers also functioned as storehouses of treasure, for the monastery's wealth and sacred objects as well as for the wealth of local nobles. Perhaps they were also last refuges during raids. In this role they were probably ineffective — a fire built at the base would turn the whole thing into a great chimney and would overcome the occupants with smoke and heat.

I am a great lover of lighthouses and as such I think the round towers are their own reason for existence. Impressive, elegant, they stand as beacons, and give me the same sense of awe and wonder and nobility of purpose as a lighthouse.

I walked clockwise around the tower, touching the ancient stones, praying, and thinking of Psalm 48 — "Walk about Zion, go all around it, count its towers, consider well its ramparts; go through its citadels. . . . "

The grounds made me uneasy as the day progressed. The sense of the dead was quite strong, and I suddenly felt keenly my mortality. In ancient days, when pilgrimage was a long and arduous journey taking months, or even years in the case of Jerusalem, it was common for pilgrims to take sick and even to die along the journey. Uneasily, I wondered how many pilgrims to Glendalough were buried beneath my feet, and whether I would want to be if I were to die here.

St. Kevin's Church often stands as an emblem of Glendalough. Oblong with a small round tower at one end, it has sometimes been called "Kevin's Kitchen," as the short tower suggests a chimney. The gate was locked when I was there. I peered inside, walked around it, but frankly did not find anything extraordinary. The interior seemed very damp and very dark. I sat and sketched the building, and blessed myself with a little standing rainwater in the hollow *bullaun* stone outside. But Kevin's Kitchen remained for me a closed door, literally and figuratively.

Hard by St. Kevin's Church are the low foundation-remains of St. Kieran's Church. Legend has it that Kevin and Kieran were soul-friends, and that Kieran attended upon Kevin's death. I liked St. Kieran's better than St. Kevin's — open and clean. Perhaps the archetypal "sky-god" open-air experience speaks to me more than the God found beneath the earth, with the shrine suggesting a cave. I stood in the low-walled ruin and prayed for the grace to be a good soul-friend to those who consider me one.

I crossed the bridge over the noisy, chuckling stream and passed the "deer stone," another of the hollowed-out bullaun stones whose original purpose has been eclipsed by their legendary use as wishing stones. This deer stone promises a granted wish to anyone who can sit upon it facing west and touch the water by stretching behind. Another blessing for those made of rubber, I muttered darkly to myself, as I blessed myself with the water that, legend says, always stands in the hollow of the stone, and walked east.

Some distance from the old "monastic city" lie another set of ruins that mark a transition in Celtic Christian life. Called St. Savior's, the ruins are those of a church and Augustinian priory founded in the high middle ages, twelfth or thirteenth century. It was built under the influence of a pivotal Irish church figure, St. Laurence O'Toole, appointed Abbot of Glendalough as well as Archbishop of Dublin. It was he along with St. Malachy, Archbishop of Armagh, who introduced reform in Irish monasteries by importing Continental religious orders, mainly Cistercians and Augustinians, to leaven by example the older Celtic monastic communities. These latter communities are often described in the official account as having become "decadent." On the one hand I can believe that — church life and history, monastic life included, is a constant cycle of decline and reform. We are now in the midst of a tremendous, traumatic time of reform ourselves, although few of us if any understand all the issues at stake and none of us know the outcome. Perhaps no one ever does at the time.

On the other hand, like the "official version" of the history of the American West that we were fed in school, replete with dastardly Indians, noble settlers, and heroic soldiers, church history was written by the victors. I wonder how "decadent" the Celtic houses really were, or whether the more individual style, diverse community membership, and "indigenous" feel of Celtic monasticism was viewed judgmentally by the eyes of the more regimented Continental monks. As the new monks had the political and military backing of the conquering Normans and those Irish allied to them, the account comes to us filtered through their eyes.

St. Savior is reached by descending a lovely bit of sloping ground carpeted with evergreen needles and pillared by the trees which drop them. There was a sense of solitude to the ruins that I liked. The ground was marshy and I received shoes full of water walking about and climbing in.

The fancy name for the architectural style is "Hiberno-Romanesque," mutely but eloquently showing the blend of old Irish and new imported Roman styles. Some lovely enigmatic carvings on some of the pillars were worth a look. The remnants of a stairway curl behind one east wall, a stairway now to nowhere. I walked up a couple of steps, but left off, afraid both of disturbing the ruins as well as of slipping and falling.

I stood and drank in the silence, which was punctuated by a boom box and some less-than-sober partying taking place somewhere in the woods off toward the river. But parenthood lets one selectively filter out a great deal. I stood and prayed and thought of the blend of Roman and Celtic in my own soul. I gave thanks for the ways in which they live together within me, albeit uneasily. And I wondered and thought about my own role in regard to reform at my own parish. The tumbled, abandoned stones seemed to say eloquently that preserving the past for its own sake is *not* a value, certainly not one that I wish to give my life to. If I wanted to be a museum curator, I would've applied to the Historical Society. On the other hand, there is great power in the past as tool, teacher, and discloser of the future, even as an object lesson for mistakes made and blind alleys to avoid.

The trees were hushed and their needles underfoot soft and yielding as I ascended the gentle rise and regained my path. I walked back west, toward the monastic city and the upper lake.

On the path I stooped and rescued a large, iridescent beetle, and sat down with him under a small rock overhang that looked like a tiny hermit's refuge. I wondered aloud if the creature was a fay, one of the "little people" in other guise. Not bothering to enlighten me, the beetle extended lacy wings and flew away.

The rain, which had been a soft whisper, decided to fall with greater power. Hunching my shoulders, I walked over the little footbridge, seeking the main stone gate of the old monastic enclosure. Expecting more of the silence of old Ireland, I emerged from the trees and was rudely dumped back into the late twentieth century.

Buses filled with elderly looking tourists were debarking their venerable cargo. A little old man stood patiently under an umbrella gaudy with the orange, white, and green of the Irish Republican flag and played a lot of "tour-a-lour-a-lour-a" stuff on an accordion. Past the buses stood a gift shop, restaurant, and a modern and pricey-looking place called the "Glendalough Hotel." I laughed aloud. I dried off in the restaurant and had a shockingly good latte. Closing my eyes, the taste of really decent coffee on my tongue, with wet feet and damp jacket, I easily imagined myself back in Portland.

The rain slackened. I got the car and drove to the car park by the upper lake. A kiosk there provided some very credible fish and chips and plenty of tea. The active part of the day felt nearly over, but there was one more stop I desired — Teampull na Maire, St. Mary's Church.

St. Mary's is visible from the center of the monastic city, part of yet strangely apart from the main complex. Not much documentation survives regarding the precise ordering of the community of Glendalough, but St. Mary's and a few whispers of tradition surrounding it suggest that it was the "women's church." Some gender-segregation at least took place at Glendalough, and perhaps St. Mary's marked the center of the feminine portion of the community. Some legends of St. Kevin suggest that sexuality and women were a sore point of struggle for him, replete with themes of temptation and heartbreaking refusal of human love. The woman who loves Kevin in one tale ends up embracing monastic life in penitence, although one popular retelling has the woman ending up drowned in the upper lake. Then there's that strange, sensual peist who amorously enwrapped Kevin's legs while he tried to recite his Psalms. It's a mistake to think we'll find in the Celtic Christians examples of people who had everything all worked out, integrated, and harmonious.

St. Mary's is best reached in a poignantly different manner than the rest of the ruins. Walk along the road, at the margin of the enclosure as it were, and climb the stile that gives access to the site.

A hush enveloped me as I entered the solitary grounds, and a sadness as well, not wrenching but pensive.

Losack and Rodgers describe a distinctive X-shaped cross that is carved into the bottom of the overhead doorway stone. One must pass under it to enter the ruined church. I kissed my fingers and touched it, and asked the ladies' permission to come in as I entered.

I stood and thought of all the women who had been gifts in my life — mothers, advisors, teachers, companions, coworkers, friends. I thanked them all.

Outside the walls of the church is a sad little patch of unmarked ground. Rodgers and Losack say that it is the place where unbaptized children were buried. I stood and grieved at the pain and anguish and violence of a theology that wouldn't give consecrated ground for the burial of innocent little ones. Thank God they were buried here, where the Mother of Christ and the women who served Christ could enfold them. The powerful eloquence and truth of motherly love speaks in a voice more authoritative than cold dogma. The women who led the marches in Northern Ireland, the mothers who stood in vigil year after year for the *desaparecidos* in Latin America, Mother Jones raising hell for the living — all and more throughout the ages knew this and practiced this, often in the face of male disdain and male fear. I smiled at all those strong women whose faces and forms invisibly ringed the church grounds.

The little ones beneath the pathetic piece of ground silently asked me for prayers, as they have asked everyone for centuries. I gave them gladly and raised my hand over them in a priest's blessing.

The rain gave me permission to take the rest of the day off. I bought some things for the family at a "woolen mill" filled with more stuff than my credit card could ever hope to handle. The pub at Laragh kept a fire going all day. Sitting with my feet propped up, sipping a Guinness, my left shoulder sweating slightly from the fragrant heat, I loved Ireland while writing lots of cards and letters. The B&B was cozy as I watched

BBC and Irish TV, read, and relaxed. "Down times" are essential on pilgrimage; one must take more rest while traveling and one cannot always be filling oneself with wonders. Often enough I found myself gazing on yet another wondrous, legendary site, but was overcome by apathy born of exhaustion. So I brooded happily that day. Glendalough did not overwhelm me as did the first day on Iona, but it was a rich and many-coursed meal of the sacred and the ancient and the simply beautiful. Digestion time was needed.

That night, a dream: I lay on a bed with a young woman, beautiful yet simple and unassuming. I looked up to see my wife walking out the door, smiling at us, assenting without rancor. The young woman embraced me, in a way that was at the same time intimate yet chaste. "At last we're alone," she whispered. I awoke feeling a strange peace.

Puzzling still over the dream, I returned to the monastic city next day.

I parked the car and walked to the crossroads cross, then back to Trinity Church. A little smugly, I found the proper way, the "narrow gate" set into the wall, and descended with more decorum than the day before. The church felt like an old friend. I noted with some amusement that my best praying seemed to happen outside of the walls of the church. I stood still in that moment of insight, a personal "aha" for me, seeing the face of Christ has mostly taken place "outside the walls" of the Church as well. I looked at the church with its roof open to the sky. The Gospel, I mused along with Losack and Rodgers, has broken forth from its old containers, just as the roof of old Trinity broke open and the clergy and people scattered. Nothing has been lost; it has only been changed.

Across the river there is a sacred well, St. Kevin's Well. I walked to it off the well-beaten path, off to the left near the river. A tree overhangs it, festooned with "clooties," traditional cloth offerings. I was charmed and heartened to see a group of teenagers at the well, hanging more cloths and, in the case of one girl, a hair-ribbon that she took from her own hair. Shyly they withdrew and walked away when I drew near.

I stared down into the sacred place. It is a natural well, with no paving or wall, overhung by a single tree. The earth around it is beaten smooth by many circling feet. The wells are one of the most concrete examples of the synthesis of the old holiness and ancient faith of the Celtic lands with the "new faith" of the Christ. The wells were sacred to the ancient Celts and were consecrated to various deities, mostly goddesses or local spirits. Archaeologists have often found treasure, weapons, and other objects in these wells by way of offerings, and the wells were often believed to have healing properties. The Christians wisely did not fill in the wells or declare them demon-haunted, but instead consecrated them to the Christ or his mother or a local saint, thereby continuing and transforming a tradition that honored the land and the faith of the people who dwell there.

I stared down into the well and felt at one and at peace. In that moment I understood my dream. It was my own soul that I had embraced and allowed to embrace me the night before, my soul that in solitude and receptivity I was finally welcoming. Gazing into the depths, the archetypal deep feminine waters, I felt deeply healed. I wondered in that moment if any of my blood kin had made the pilgrimage to Glendalough and had prayed at this well. I circled it *diseal*, clockwise, praying the while. I tied my own cloth to the tree and bowed to St. Kevin, touching my forelock with respect to any other benign spirit who lingered there in this disenchanted and single-dimensional age. Regaining the path, I walked on.

The day was clear and bright, and I sweated slightly in my layers. Past the bridge to the monastic city, past the deer stone, more people walked or lingered on the path. The bulk of them seemed to be Irish folk, mostly retired-looking, and some young families with children. Also there were young adults, very fit and attractive, from whom I heard snatches of various languages. But as I walked, either smiling or engaging in the delicate art of noninteraction with people whom you almost bump into, I was aware that the path was even more crowded. Unseen pilgrims jostled the living as I walked up the well-marked path along the lakeshore.

By the upper lake is a series of fields, marked with small, worn stone crosses, and including a stone circle that is now called the Caher. No one knows its purpose — an ancient fortified dwelling perhaps? But I stood within it and felt encircled and safe.

The fields within which lies the Caher became the gathering place for the throngs who made the "pattern," the pilgrimage to Glendalough.

For those who could manage it, the journey ended when the pilgrim lay upon the stones of "Kevin's Bed" in the dank cave at the side of the upper lake. It's difficult to get there now — the bluff is very steep and dangerous to descend in order to reach the cave from above, and no boats regularly ply the dark waters of the upper lake to cross and gain access as they did in former times. I think the reasoning is twofold — the journey to Kevin's Bed, including the cave itself, presents some hazards, and although it would be difficult to sue St. Kevin there is a sense of responsibility for the unlucky or inept pilgrim. Also, restricting access to the far shore makes the stone remnants of the community of hermit monks on the far shore and Kevin's Bed itself a place of mystery, a "far shore" that one glimpses in prayer, a promise and a destination not to be reached in this life. And then there's the matter of the peist. As peist-repellant is not readily available retail, I left the water to him.

I walked and touched tenderly the stone scraps and remnants of the old pilgrim gatherings slumbering in the grass: a fragment of a stone cross, the foundations of what might have been a small chapel or shrine. I felt with gratitude the presence of the lusty men and women who had gathered for centuries to make the pattern, who walked, prayed, ate, sang, fought, and made love along the way.

I walked on to the ruins at the head of the lake on a rise — Reefert Church.

Reefert, Rodgers and Losack report, by tradition is called the "burial place of kings." I found it solemn and hushed, positively paved with graves. I walked gingerly, not yet able to be so familiar with the dead as to tramp over their beds. There were lovely, worn Celtic carvings on the stones, and a great standing ringed cross.

Within the ruined church was hush and prayer. I stood in stillness, and in that moment felt unexpectedly close to my mother and my father, and to grandmother Bridie and to Patrick and to baby Thomas. I wondered at that, wondered if a place like Reefert functions as the spiritual burial place of all Ireland, and whether each people on the face of the earth are blessed with such a place where the spirits of their dead may be found. I thought of the Black Hills in South Dakota, and how for the Lakota it is a spirit-place and a sacred place. No one with a soul can experience the sacred ground of their God and their people and ever disregard the sacred ground of others.

I shook off speculation and prayed for my own dead.

I was not alone at Reefert even among the living. A German couple exploring the ruins exited the grounds on the way toward Kevin's Cell. They figured out the stile over the wall, and I followed. I walked slowly so as to allow them to draw ahead.

The sun dappled the woods, and the path came suddenly to a raised circular space, small, ringed with a wall of low cut stones, with small saplings here and there in the wall. Tradition calls this the remains of Kevin's Cell.

It's in the right place for it, I thought, here near the upper lake, secluded yet accessible, somewhat like the "retreat hut" of the Methodist conference center near my home. It was easy to imagine the corbelled dry-stone walls atop the humble foundation.

I sat upon the wall with a strong sense that I had arrived at another destination point of my pilgrimage. I reached into my backpack and pulled forth the book of prayers and petitions from my parishioners. I opened it and spread it out for Kevin to see. And Kevin the abbot and I had a conversation.

I had no previous devotion to St. Kevin and, truth to tell, to this day he does not capture my imagination as do Brigid and Columba. But I was filled with gratitude that he had so generously shared his life and his sacred ground with me, and was eager to hear what he had to say.

He mostly listened. I told him of my parish, my life, the crossroads at which I felt myself and my ministry. I prayed for the parish and he prayed with me.

I surprised myself by asking him to pray that I might be chaste according to my state in life. And I asked him to teach me to pray, especially in the old desert way of which he was so clearly fond.

Kevin is gentle and patient. As I talked and he listened, I had the image of two abbots meeting and speaking of their lives; this image appears often in Irish literature and in stone carving. The thought occurred to me strangely — am I then an abbot?

My time was up. I bid Kevin farewell and walked on.

The path up into the woods is beautiful and still. I walked and breathed, smiled upon meeting a lively looking group of local teenagers in orange pinneys, doing something commendably ecological and useful with plastic bags. The path passed by a lovely waterfall called Poulanass. I stood on the narrow bridge and drank in the music of the waters. I thought of that day years before in Japan, in Nara, when my guide led me onto a small footbridge and asked me to listen to the rushing water. "That's *kimuchi*," he assured me, a difficult-to-translate word roughly meaning "Japanese-ness."

I walked back down, to the shoreline of the upper lake, and there re-entered my own world with a vengeance.

In the midst of the small, windswept lake, an ungainly looking ship thrashed at its anchor rope, two men hauling at the rope like wild horse breakers, getting nowhere. On the shore, other men busily hammered on a strange structure, which looked like a house and yet was strangely partial and incomplete. I sauntered up to a harried-looking man who looked as if he felt he needed to be in charge and asked him what all the activity was.

He looked at me with weary surprise. "It's a set," he assured me in strangely unaccented English. "We're filming a commercial for Capital One. Have you heard of them?"

What's in *your* wallet? I thought to myself with grim humor. Capital One was at the time one of the credit card companies that owned me and my household. I thanked the man and strolled on, chuckling while eyeing the strange hulk on the dark waters. Where's a peist when you need one, I thought, hoping that Kevin's beast would at least have the decency to chew through the anchor rope that night.

I found a sunlit place on the shore of the lake, along what my map called the Miner's Road, and looked over at the remains of the hermit community on the far shore. It was that little collection of huts and standing crosses that made clear to me the empathy and continuity between Celtic monasticism and that of the deserts of North Africa and Palestine. There was the *lavra*, the tiny huts clustered so as to protect both solitude and community. The tiny refuge seemed to me to be the heart of the Glendalough community. And above, a dark spot on the cliffside, was the cave housing Kevin's Bed.

I sat and thought of mortality and new life and solitude. I thought of the many times I had journeyed alone to places, and of the vulnerability in that experience. The cave mouth was not only still, but seemed to me to be the source of the stillness of the valley. Make a still place in me, I prayed.

I stopped along the shore of the lower lake on the way back. I took from my pocket a rock that I had been carrying. I placed all my anxiety, fear, and shame on the rock and, saying a prayer, hurled it far out into the water. The lake took it without a quiver.

As I took my way home along the Green Road, I stopped and stared. A staff leaned against a tree, a long, sturdy, natural branch. Some hiker, I thought, leaving their walking stick behind. But as I stared, I remembered the custom among Celtic abbots of one giving a staff to another to symbolize their authority to lead a community. I reached out and took the staff. The top was smooth to my hand. Hitting a good stride, I walked all the way back to the bridge leading into the monastic city. There I leaned the staff against a tree for someone else to use. But I do believe I carry that staff still.

Laragh and Glendalough were cozy and safe places to be. I stayed on a couple more days.

Looking for a way to wash clothes, I drove miles down the road to an attractive village. I learned that day that the notion of a laundromat and washing one's own clothes is untraditional, that there are laundries and launderettes to do this for you. I smiled at the ladies and mentioned "my beautiful launderette," and they rewarded me with lovely Irish smiles and questions about who I was and what I was doing. When I told them I was a pilgrim in Glendalough, they eagerly told me that I simply had to meet "lovely Father Mike" who "helps all the people who come." They told me how to find Michael Rodgers.

Michael's retreat house is a secluded little group of buildings just above the road from Laragh. I'm afraid I bothered the poor man trying to rest, but he greeted me with typical Irish hospitality. He invited me to Eucharist and dinner with the rest of the pilgrims staying there. They were a welcoming bunch. A charming Japanese nun told me that Glendalough heals her in her Japanese-ness, and was moved when I told her of my *kimuchi* experience by the waterfall.

In private, I told Michael of finding all that fuss and bother and clutter by the upper lake, the Capital One set and all. He was visibly disturbed, saying that the upper lake is a natural treasure, a religious shrine, and part of Ireland's cultural heritage all at once, and shooting a commercial there is an example of what is being lost amidst Ireland's new "Celtic Tiger" prosperity.

I looked at the dear man and felt in my own soul the loss of so much that is sacred amidst the vast market that is today's world.

"Michael, just say the word," I said. "You know Glendalough like the back of your hand. We'll slip in, burn that ridiculous ship to the waterline, and be back here sipping tea before anyone notices."

The lovely man was silent for a few moments. Finally he looked up and thanked me, but merely said, "They'll be gone soon."

Subversive impulses aside, I went home blessed by their hospitality and cheered by the oasis of company. I delighted in the unspoken understanding that pilgrims give one another as gift.

The autumn was advancing, and the spider's webs outside the window of the B&B were sparkling with frost. The clouds built slowly and promised more rain. As cozy as was Glendalough, it was time to leave.

chapter 17

town of tears
and bloody stones

As I CRUISED through the lovely Wicklow Gap, the rain first threatened then began to pelt the windshield. The map was true and the roads clear, and so I arrived in New Ross, the town of my grandparents.

I had been filled with stories of the place, yet did not know in the least what to expect. New Ross is far from any romance of the picture-perfect Irish village where an old man recognizes your name in the pub, tells you all about your family, and the whole pub buys you a pint and sings to you.

The family stories were of a poverty-stricken town, and I expected something quite small.

The New Ross of the twenty-first century is, however, a bustling and vital place, not an Irish postcard for the tourists, but booming housing and exurb development enclosing the buildings of the grim old town like a plush pillow enveloping a rough gray stone. Traffic teemed, especially at the rush hour times at the beginning and the close of the day. Two-story suburban-style houses nestled as close to the old town's outskirts as they dared. People on the streets were brisk and busy, and never did I see anyone just "hanging out" except in the older pubs.

I drove to the heart of the old town and looked for the tourist board. The B&B recommended by the guidebook, right in the heart of the old town, was full, and besides, I thought that the building front looked grim and depressing. I drove to another, and did the owners a favor by giving their hedge a good trim with the left side of the car as I drove up the drive. The owner and his wife, speaking in what sounded like German accents, told me they were closed for the season, but brought me into their kitchen and kindly called around until they found me a room. I left and drove out of the center of town and fetched up at a brand-new suburban place called Oakwood House. A nice lady named Sue and her husband, a retired Garda (police), greeted me graciously. At first I felt awkward that I was staying at a place not even dreamed of when my grandparents were in New Ross. But I forgave myself enjoying the suburban comforts of Oakwood House. Sue was kind and motherly, often sitting down with a cup of tea and hearing me out about the day's plans or its adventures when it was over. Her husband also kindly listened and punctuated my remarks with an occasional small gasp of empathy, done with a brief intake of breath. I came to love that mannerism, and began to notice it in other local folks. The Irish have a masterful way of giving you their hearts.

I spent almost a week in New Ross. I was surprised that I did. I realized that I was searching for my family, and I was searching for lost Bridie and Patrick especially. My mother's tales had graven themselves more deeply on my soul than I had ever imagined. The sense of being lost and alone that she conveyed and carried throughout her life had become my own. I roamed the streets restlessly, even anxiously. I hoped to pick a face out of the crowd, one that I would know or that would know me beyond reason or hope. I wanted to find Patrick and Bridie, something — a stone, a sign, a story. I needed to know that they were not lost forever, vanished in the slums of turn-of-the-century Manhattan, then buried in pauper's graves.

The stress of it was plain on my face. I did meet God one day, and he was drunk. I emerged from a pub that had re-imagined itself as a yuppie fast-pub-food sort of place, where you order lunch lined up and take a plastic tray. At least the Guinness was served in a real glass. God was a large, florid, black-haired fellow making his way merrily along the sidewalk when I walked out. He caught my eye, spread his arms wide and commanded, "Don't look so lost, man! Enjoy yourself!"

I worked hard on getting myself un-lost, although it did occur to me, standing on the sidewalk and absorbing my spiritual direction for the day, that a few more pints of Guinness would accomplish the same faster and be more fun. No doubt plenty of my kin had gotten loaded on that very street, and had cured any sense of being lost for a few hours at least.

Like its larger neighbor Wexford, New Ross was in all likelihood a Viking settlement. It was the Norse who built the first towns, ports for trading and raiding the interior. Then the Normans came ashore here or very near here, led by William Le Clare, known as "Strongbow." He imported Benedictine monks from Normandy, again evicting a Celtic monastic community in order to build his abbey and accomplishing his domination of the local church. The ruins of the Norman abbey are still in use as St. Mary's Church, the nave surviving but the transepts and apse in ruins and open to the sky. As usual, the Anglicans have the old church and the Roman Catholics, exponentially many times their number, have a much newer church on the other side of town.

I found the abbey grounds early in my stay.

It is a wonderfully weedy and overgrown place, in spite of some valiant efforts by local folks to keep it in order by volunteer labor. The graves, going back to medieval burials, crowd in one upon another just as at Glendalough. The open-roofed cruciform transept is also paved with ancient graves. It was wonderful and ghastly and delightful and oppressive all at once. A lady down the road kept the key to the gates and also to the locked vaults under the church. And I, even I, who love a good haunted spot with plenty of Gothic atmosphere and lurid stories, looked in at the opened wall vaults and the sarcophagi lying open on the floor and shuddered. It was not so much the prospect of encountering a spectre that concerned me so much as the air of finality and death that oppressed me. But still I roamed the grounds, peering at stones and touching them, treating them like a rare book that I was being allowed to page. The burying ground was used for more than historical reference, as I could see — broken booze bottles, cans, and the occasional used condom spoke eloquently of time-honored use by the living.

Popping up like some aged sprite, the lady of the key appeared and let me into the roofless transepts and crossing of the church. Pointing to a once-lovely sarcophagus lying on the ground, she assured me that folk roundabout knew it was the sarcophagus of Lady Strongbow, William Le Clare's wife. "And would you like to try it on for size?"

Bemused, I asked, "And why would I be doin' that?"

She shrugged. "Some of the boys and girls think it's something to do. And they say that if you do so, something will happen."

"And what is that?"

"I don't know, but whatever it is, it's not good."

Lady Strongbow's sarcophagus lies there still insofar as I know, never having known my bones or flesh. I figured I had no need to court any bad luck on my travels.

A gentle-looking old man walked his little dogs about the graves, occasionally glancing at me shyly, then looking hastily away. I thought of the enduring reputation for shyness that leprechauns enjoy. Eventually, our Celtic knot-work of paths intersected, and his shyness ended as we began to talk.

Joe, as he named himself, turned out to be a trove of lore. His face crinkled in a nearly perpetual smile that brought life and joy to that lugubrious place. Upon my telling him my family history and the family names, Joe told me that Flood had been the older name in town, and spoke of a John Flood and his wife who had lived there until twenty or thirty years before. They owned a pub in a little section of town named "Flood's Lane." More Floods lived out in the countryside, as well as out in Tramore on the coast, and in Kilkenny. He told me that the Floods he knew were Catholic, which cast me down a bit. If Patrick had been Protestant, it would explain a great deal of the Morrissey family rejection. I also wanted the Protestant connection so as to make sense of my personal history, and why I found moving from Rome to Canterbury a natural sort of thing.

Joe told me that the Morrissey's were relative late-comers to the town. They lived out in "Irishtown," the portion of the town literally beyond "the Pale," an archaic word for "wall." Joe also referred to "the Murragh," but I couldn't get whether that was another name for the boundary or for the Irishtown district. Like many another older city, the built-up center of New Ross was a stronghold of the English and the Anglo-Irish Protestants. A fortified stone wall, gated and fitted with crenellations for artillery and muskets, separated this "civilized" portion from the Catholic and poorer section of town. Hence the expression "Beyond the Pale."

At least in those days they were more frank and honest, and built a wall that one could see. Today's walls between haves and have-nots are no less strong but are largely invisible. They are no less well-guarded.

Joe told me of a shop downtown that the Morrisseys owned, where they sold "pins and such." I mentioned fishing to him, and Joe said there used to be salmon in the river. People used to set nets for the salmon from little flat-bottomed boats called "cots." The nets would be set between two boats, which would move together, closing the net and trapping the salmon, "Snap" said Joe, clapping his hands. The salmon left, Joe continued, when the English-owned factory upstream polluted the river. What I had seen of the river looked none too clean even now, so I easily imagined the end of the salmon runs and the people having nothing, nothing, grass and dirt and empty bellies and no work and the remnants of the mercantile aristocracy living in the stone houses or out on the estates and caring little if anything for the commoners. No wonder people left. No wonder that any life overseas was better than no life.

When the salmon failed, when there was nothing but the useless little boats and the empty rotting nets and growling bellies, in desperation they decided to leave. Were Patrick and Bridie married yet? If not, did Patrick choose to follow Bridie into exile? The family tale said Patrick "tended bar" in NYC — did he first learn to "pull beers" at the pub on Flood's Lane, where the great wooden levers forced the black ale out of its cask and into the glass?

Joe showed me a map of the graveyard. We saw a grave marked "Flood," and we combed the weedy grounds excitedly until we found it. The stone was cheap and badly eroded, almost illegible. The burial was from sometime in the early nineteenth century. Joe told me that the older graves were Catholic, the newer Protestant. Among the graves, he said, were those of two Royal Navy midshipmen killed on the streets in Wolfe Tone's uprising of 1798.

I found their graves and shuddered again, knowing that the midshipmen were very likely young men, very young — eighteen or so, and maybe as young as twelve or thirteen. Midshipmen were apprentice officers and their commissions were "starter" positions. Talented, ambitious boys would not spend more than a few years as "middies," taking their exams to qualify as lieutenants as soon as they had enough experience and knowledge. For all their youth, they were often in the thick of any fighting that occurred. I looked with pity upon the two graves and thought of the two boys, not much older than my son at the time, who perished on howling bloody streets so long ago.

In this same year one of Ireland's poet-politicians, Theobald Wolfe Tone, helped organize a grand plan to raise Ireland against the British while Mother England was preoccupied with Napoleon in Europe. Napoleon was approached by the rebels and agreed to land troops in Ireland while Wolfe Tone and his fellow rebels rallied the country. The mass of armed and organized peasants, supported by French troops, would sweep away the English garrisons and would establish a free Ireland, hostile to England, friendly to France, surrounding Britain with enemies.

But win-win propositions were just as treacherous in the eighteenth century as they are today. The French troops were dispatched on ships but most never landed — amphibious operations of the day were notoriously unreliable and were even more subject to weather than they are today. But Wolfe Tone and the rest went ahead and raised the countryside. New Ross became the scene for the Battle of New Ross, one of the climactic battles of the revolt.

Joe, who had left with his dogs, shyly returned to the yard holding his car keys like a mouse held by its tail. He offered to drive me to the other, newer cemetery, and I accepted.

This place was far more neat and kempt, obviously a working cemetery busy with the polite rituals of organized death and mourning. Joe pointed out some huge and gaudy graves, called them "gypsy." After the English arrived, he explained, people were commonly forced off their land by economic hardship or eviction, and would stay together, living in caravans of horse-drawn trailers. Even now, when these clans had prospered somewhat, they kept to their lifestyle of living in caravans, now mobile homes, or RVs, which had become for them their family tradition.

Joe took his leave and I walked among the graves. Finally I found one labeled "Morrissey," took a picture, and noted the address thoughtfully listed beneath the date on the stone. I smiled at the thought of the dead providing their own directory listing, and took my leave to walk back to town.

I shared the road with a sprightly elderly woman who clearly could walk me into the ground if she so chose. She peered suspiciously at the outlandish stranger sharing her accustomed way, but after a few dozen yards she responded to my smiles and slowed down. When I told her a bit of my tale, she told me of a shop owned by a man named Cleary, who knew the Floods of Flood Lane.

I kept my road leading down and into the old town, and soon passed a monument set in the middle of the road, topped with a broken Celtic cross. "Irishtown," said the bronze plaque. Then, a crumbling remnant of natural stone wall — the Pale, a small cannon, and a mural on a building facing the wall depicting a young man with a tall, pointed spear — a pike — looking at old New Ross as the sun set.

Wolfe Tone's Irish peasantry had few muskets or other arms. But they had wooden staves with wicked forged metal spearheads — pikes. In that day, when firearms were still clumsy, muzzle-loading single-shot affairs, a determined body of people with pikes, fighting in a disciplined formation, could overwhelm soldiers armed with muskets, if they were willing to accept some dreadful losses. One volley, the barely aimed lead musket balls sweeping away a line of people, maybe another volley, and perhaps a third if the troops were extraordinarily disciplined and skilled. But by then the remnants of the pike-armed people would be among them, battle-mad and further inflamed by the loss of their friends. Fumbling with their bayonets, the troops would then be in an even fight with people wielding one of the oldest and most effective close-in weapons in the world.

The bronze plaque on the wall said that the pike-men had gotten as far as that point on the first day. Perhaps they had actually taken the wall until darkness and exhaustion and losses had stopped them. The defenders, probably frightened and demoralized, had fled to the next line of defense.

The streets became steep, and the cobblestones were slick from the morning dew. I shuddered as I concentrated on keeping my footing. No doubt back in those dread days the stones were slick with blood.

Only a few blocks further down, a second plaque, set in the ground, marked "Day two — the pike-men advanced this far." What a laconic way to describe the howls, the blood, bodies piled up from the musket-volleys, the terror. Did the Anglo-Irish think they would ever get out, ever survive, as the howling pike-men swept down upon them as Celtic warriors always had upon their enemies?

"Day three," said another plaque on a wall. I looked up and saw the stone building at the heart of town.

The remnants of the sailors and soldiers and the Anglo-Irish loyalists had holed up in this building, trapped at last. They mounted swivel guns from the ships moored in the river at the corner windows, and fired with desperation down the streets. Wave after wave, the pikes came, died and withdrew. The British somehow held out. The rebellion, fueled by raw nerve and determination and hate, faltered and died on those streets. The rest of the story of Wolfe Tone's revolt was a matter of hunting and reprisals, of courts and executions.

Opposite the old building stands a life-sized statue of "The Pikeman." He gazes still with defiance and longing upon the building he never took and will never enter.

Ah yes. My old home town. What was it like to live and grow up here amidst the stones and the sad monuments of savagery?

If we're lucky, we weary of war and reprisals. As I walked, I saw William's face back in Belfast as he drove down the Falls Road, "Most of us just want peace."

And so I looked for Bridie and Patrick. I did so with an anxiety that surprised me. It was as if they were in imminent peril, or as if it were my personal job to seek them out, any trace of them, and tell the tale, so that the young couple who died a pauper's death in New York City would not be as if they never were. Only in a misty fashion did I understand that I was seeking to heal my mother's sense of being lost and alone on the face of the earth, an orphan. Even less clear was that I was looking to heal my own sense of being lost. Of all my brothers, I was the one who felt and lived most deeply a sense of rootlessness and exile. Perhaps I took the old stories far too much to heart.

One oasis of sun and light came from the town's Roman Catholic church.

I felt in deep need of the Eucharist, of Communion, and so went to the Roman Catholic parish's Saturday evening Mass. I sat in the vast interior of the church and dandled my rosary piously while a good-sized congregation gathered. The stocky young priest spoke movingly of loss and brokenness and alienation in families in his homily. It occurred to me to seek him out and ask him if he wanted to go somewhere for a pint, but I dismissed the idea. Most of the men I spoke with at length told me they were trying to "get away from the stuff," testifying to the endemic Irish alcoholism that is the shadow-side of the jolly Irish pub. I suspect many of the priests are in recovery themselves or feel they should set something of an example. I left the church alone, feeling envious of those who left with family or friends.

Two days later I called ahead and kept an appointment at the huge, hulking brick rectory. I wanted to search the parish records for family. Treating my request as very ordinary, the young priest and the secretary greeted me warmly as "Father." They showed me to a large, comfortable old parlor with a large table, and the lady brought me a pot of tea and some biscuits. The young priest emerged bearing not a stack of moldy crumbling registers as I expected, but large ringed binders stuffed full of computer printouts. He explained that the Irish Roman Catholic Church, constantly besieged by expatriate Irish descendants looking for genealogical information, had called in all parish records that had survived the vicissitudes of time and had made a massive database, giving each parish a hard copy of its own records neatly organized. I was relieved at the ease of my task, yet a little let down that I would not be peering at ancient scrawl on yellowed pages.

I found out a great deal. I found out that Bridie had not been the youngest, but the second oldest. I found out a lot about the Powers clan, Bridie's mother who had by family story vindictively burned every picture of Patrick and every document bearing his name. And I found that Bridie had a brother, who had gone off to Australia, that other port of refuge for the Wild Geese, about the same time that Bridie and Patrick had left Ireland. I found no record of their marriage — was it at another location close by, or in New York?

I chuckled as I went down the list of parish births. The old registers had a column in which the priest made note of the marital status of each child's parents. A sizeable portion of the births of the time were labeled "illegitimate." Centuries of Roman Catholicism could not wholly domesticate the Celtic hormones, God bless 'em. It's the human in us which Christ loves dear.

The Anglicans provided another oasis.

I had to make a good guess at Sunday service times for the Church of Ireland congregation meeting in the ancient nave of St. Mary's. No sign with service times was posted, no information was available save the word of old Joe and the key-lady, who scratched their heads and said they seen the Anglicans from time to time, "about ten" or thereabouts of a Sunday. I showed up about 9:45 and found an open door.

A congregation of about thirty-five souls sat in the nave, the walls lined with large memorial plaques, all very old-line Protestant with no images of saints. A hearty priest led a service that involved a lot of singing and recited prayers, no Communion. But it was good to feel the Anglican part of my soul connected with other denominational tribal members. After the service, I sauntered out looking forward to coffee hour and a chance to meet some folks, only to see the last soul disappear down the sidewalk. No cookies and tea at St. Mary's Church of Ireland on a Sunday, at least not at the church.

The priest was still there, and we talked at length and commiserated as do clergy everywhere. I was delighted to find another expatriate soul. The vicar proved to be a Yank, an ex–Roman Catholic priest of the Columban Missionaries, old friends of mine from Chicago. He had left his order, married a Korean woman, and had been accepted into the Church of Ireland. As we spoke, his two charming kids ran up, and in delightful Irish brogues asked Daddy for "some pence for sweeties." The living reality of the global village made my head swim, and I smiled as I watched the kids scamper out of the ancient graveyard in search of tooth decay material.

I took a break to look for a saint I had never heard of.

Marcus Losack had kindly met me back in Glendalough's incongruously elegant hotel restaurant to give me some pilgrim pointers. He told me where to find the finest High Crosses: "Moone and Castledermot, but don't miss Monasterboise; it's the jewel in the crown. And then there's Ardmore. St. Declan, a predecessor to Patrick, a pilgrim path and round tower and well. I hear it's worth seeing. I haven't, so let me know what you think." With some relief I quit my distracted roaming of New Ross and, on a day with intermittent rain, drove the car west, through congested Waterford, to find Ardmore, nestled against a curve of beach on the south coast.

Patrick did not technically "bring Christianity" to Ireland. Another bishop named Palladius had preceded him, and stories tell of other monks and holy folk. Declan was supposedly educated in Gaul, where he was steeped in the transplanted African monastic ideal. Declan's was very much a "desert" foundation, as he sought to make his "place of resurrection" at what was the isolated fastness of Ard-Mohr, "Great Rock." Declan's memory is well-preserved in the sight of his monastic settlement, which include a round tower and the ruins of Ardmore Cathedral, surrounded by the usual welter of graves. Declan's Well is on the site of what is thought to have been his hermitage or *diseart*, near to a trail along a cliff-edge overlooking the Irish Sea where the wondrous desolation and solitude of the coast can be tasted in all its glory. As it was a chilly and wet weekday in October, I had the place almost wholly to myself.

I parked the car and found the parish church. The local priest had made a project of reviving and interpreting the old "pattern" of Declan for pilgrims. Armed with a nicely written booklet, I walked to the head of the pilgrim trail.

A large bas-relief of Declan marks the entrance. The low stone structure topped with a cross covering Declan's Well was etched with numerous crosses scratched by pilgrims. I added my own, and began to walk about the small natural cloister of the diseart, saying the prayers prescribed in the booklet and adding my own.

The waves sighed below. The air positively *smelled* green, and the riot of undergrowth around me teemed with insect life which hummed and rustled. Hearing the bursting vitality of life, filling my nose and lungs again and again with the green air, I thought that it was one thing to read and think about Celtic spirituality. But it was another thing to be breathing it, tasting it on the air, hearing it, feeling it yield and give and spring back underfoot.

I left the diseart, the well and ruined chapel, and took the path along the cliff.

It is really a gentle walk, not to be missed although not to be danced with one's eyes closed, lest your bones become a permanent part of the streaming rocks below. As I walked, solitude — not loneliness but solitude — manifested itself to me. It was a solitude that promised to somehow lift the veil over something in my soul or in the world's soul. Solitude enveloped me and bore me up. The cliff-walk is timeless, and even the shards of the modern age such as a wrecked work-ship on the rocks below or a World War II–era concrete watch station do nothing to diminish the sense of walking in an ancient dream. I prayed and thought and breathed, utterly at peace.

The trail ended in the old monastic enclosure, where the round tower, the ruined cathedral, and the sunken chapel which once housed the bones of Declan all lay. I touched and circled the tower, taking comfort in its solidity. The cathedral is a treasure-trove of carving. On its walls are found an Epiphany carving, and within an Ogham stone, edged with the strange cryptic tree-branch script of another time.

I stooped and cleaned up the remnants of broken booze bottles by the Ogham stone. Another visitor, an Englishman who told me he comes to Ardmore for "the peace," saw me and said, "Good on you." He stood me a drink in the pub and we chatted of what we both sought in such an out-of-the-way place. Other than "peace," we never quite found a common tongue, although we had a relaxing time searching for one. This was one of the times when I met a man and sensed in him a vague, inarticulate hunger, something for which he longed that he thought I, a stranger and outlander, could somehow assuage. In this instance I sensed a longing for companionship coupled with a curiosity about what motivated me. But I found myself inarticulate about my deeper motivations and that I simply lacked the energy to respond to another's spiritual need. I noted this with interest, wondering from time to time if this meant that my days as a clergyman were drawing to an end and that I was not meant to be "on" for other people's spiritual or emotional needs any more. Now I think that I was a true pilgrim and that I was "over there" out of my own poverty and need of soul and it was not the time to be helping anyone else. I also think that there was something else that I was supposed to learn. Clergy are constantly surrounded by needy people, who look to us for scraps of meaning and healing and significance. My doctor, who numbers several clergy among his patients, says from his perspective that everyone who walks in the door, or calls, or in this day e-mails, wants a bite of us clergy, so that at the end of the average day we feel like the edge of a postage stamp, ragged with bites. It is easy and treacherous to make no distinction between giving of ourselves and the fact that it is the divine that people want, they want God, they want the Christ, they want meaning and healing and significance and hope and transcendence and all that the great God-shaped hole within each of us yearns and cries out for. As such, before long my conversation with the friendly British man sputtered to a stop, and so I thanked him for the pint and bid him farewell.

Ardmore was not beautiful but striking and powerful in the gray and the wet, much prettier I am sure in the sunlight, with the lovely history and heritage of ancient Declan and his lonely, longed-for desert. But leaving town I could see the faint but unmistakable hallmarks of Small Town Anywhere, and imagined the young people who may well fret and fidget and dream of seeing the wide world and anyplace other and bigger and more happenin' than dreary little old Ardmore. So we long for someone else's perceived paradise.

Each saint thus far had taught me something, given me a lasting gift. Columba had taught me vision, and struggle as the way of the inner warrior, the "island soldier" of Christ. Patrick taught me courage. Kevin of Glendalough taught me leadership and prayer. Declan taught me solitude. To this day, closing my eyes is all it takes to find myself on the narrow lonely trail along the cliff-edge. It comforts me and makes me shiver all at once. To know solitude is to know smallness and mortality. But only then is faith possible, only then does hope become real.

Returning to New Ross was like coming home. I found a pub, an older place by the outskirts of town, a sort of stucco place old enough to have seen some of my ancestors. Good parking, just enough local folks to eye me shyly and warily until I smiled at them, then the Irish hospitality burst forth effusively. "You on holiday, then?"

But I sensed my last days there had come.

I bought a rather pricey book called *Celtic and Early Christian Wexford* in what looked like the only bookstore in town (one disappointment for me was the lack of bookstores in the smaller Irish towns, but maybe I didn't know where to look). The proprietor told me that the photography shop down the street was one of the oldest businesses and had a fine collection of photos from "the old days."

I found far more than a shop full of old pictures.

Inside the nicely remodeled shop was a trove of images from New Ross gone by. The same streets I had walked were pictured, but devoid of the teeming late-model cars that jam them now. Faces were mostly gaunt and hungry, with that look of forced aimlessness borne by those with no work. I stood before a photo of the street onto which "Flood Lane," the tiny alley next to the old Flood-owned pub, opened out. There were pushcarts and small horse-carts, some period-clad men standing idle, the grim government building where the desperate British held off the pike-men — but no visible activity, nothing to break up the sense of emptiness and gray. The photo felt like a vortex that drew me in, and a brief irrational thought about time-travel crossed my mind. I shook off what felt mad even to me and bought the framed picture.

The young proprietor seemed accustomed to dealing with questing Yanks, and we talked about the old town and its history, the memory of which the shopkeeper was determined to keep alive through the photos. Presently he said, "There's someone here you want to be meeting." He walked over to a set of stairs and shouted up, "Dad! Hey, Dad! Someone to meet you." A few moment's silence, then down the stairs, two feet on each step, a hesitation, then two feet on the next, walked the Rosetta Stone.

He was a magnificent old man, erect and tall, with a white handlebar mustache, dressed in an immaculate three piece suit and tie, a cup and saucer of coffee balanced carefully in his hand as if it were the Holy Grail.

The young shopkeep shouted, "Hey Dad! Remember the Floods?"

"Floods, yes. I remember. Water up to here...."

"No Dad, the Floods, the family."

Slowly the venerable fellow's lined face changed. Comrades who were dust in their still graves awoke and moved among his furrows.

"Flood, Flood, John Flood. Had the pub and eatery down the way. His son, John Flood too. They sent him to university. Only he didn't go to school. Just stayed down in Dublin. Then he came back. You, now," he said, peering at me suspiciously. "What have you to do with the Floods?"

I explained to him that my grandfather was a Flood, and grandmother a Morrissey.

"Morrissey, Morrissey. I don't know. Morrissey, Morrissey..." he chanted, a kind of mantra, a psalm, a sutra invoking memory of the dead. He peered again at me, not willing to satisfy impertinent curiosity, "What have you to do with Morrisseys?"

I explained again, feeling like I was being posed the Three Questions of the Grail.

"Morrissey, Morrissey. Larry Morrissey. Wore a brown coat, heavy. Stood in that doorway, there," pointing across the street.

I mentioned fishing.

"Yes, the fishing. Those from town, fished below the bridge. Those from Irishtown, from the Maudlins, fished above. By Morrissey's Bank."

I startled violently. "What?"

"Morrissey's Bank. By the old brewery, there before the old railway bridge. This side of the river. Morrissey, Morrissey. Lived in the Maudlins, would come over Goat Hill, through the Little Wood, to Morrissey's Bank. The cots, they called the boats. Little flat-bottomed. They worked in pairs, with the nets. At the salmon."

Excitedly, I interrupted, "This is just want I wanted to know!"

He looked at me reproachfully. "Not fair to just come in unannounced, jump me with questions, couldn't prepare at all."

I apologized hurriedly, terrified that the stream of story would run dry, "But you're doing great."

"Morrissey, Morrissey," he sighed. "In Irishtown, in the Maudlins. A shop here too — sold clothes and pins. Morrissey, Larry Morrissey."

I told him that Patrick and Bridie's marriage had been disapproved of, and what did he think of that?

He sighed. "Class, probably. People were very class-conscious. They could've thought he was beneath them. They had nothing, but they were proud. They would resent one another.

"You've drained me dry," he said reproachfully, but with a twinkle in his eye.

"I thank you most kindly."

He drew himself erect and smiled proudly. "One thing you've proven to me: my memory is as good as it was forty years ago!"

He paused. "Did they keep pigs?"

I almost ran from the shop, down the streets to a dirt lane with an abandoned feel, down to the riverbank. A forlorn feeling came over me, a mourning, as the forgotten path unwound slowly ahead. A tight little cottage on the left, looking inhabited and modernized behind a high fence. Large crumbling ruins lay ahead, through which I passed via an intact attractive arched doorway — the brewery, or what was left of it.

Where the ruins ended, the river lapped at greasy stones and mud. Nearby were the remnants of the railway bridge. Morrissey's Bank. The romantic stories of my mother and aunt had conjured images of a whole village, or at least docks and quays.

A patch of muddy riverbank it was, desolate and forlorn. Simple people, fishing to eat and live. Little boats called "cots." Crossing the Goat Hill, that rose behind my right shoulder. Through the Little Wood, still there. Morrissey's Bank. Gone to America and Australia, as the wild geese fly, gone to graves and stories.

> ... *their days are like grass;*
> *they flourish like a flower of the field;*
> *for the wind passes over it, and it is gone,*
> *and its place knows it no more.*
>
> (Psalm 103:15–16)

On Morrissey's Bank, perhaps the last Morrissey-descendent to stand there in many a long year, right then I think I understood what it means to be Irish, to trace my roots and blood to that place and time. To work and sweat, to struggle against oblivion, fighting it off like a river's floodwaters, shaking a fist at the dark. To know pride, even in defeat and death. To never, ever give in. To never surrender sweet life and dignity without a fight. To have the courage to begin again, even if beginning means exile and a strange new land.

They didn't do too badly, the old folks, those old Floods and Morrisseys and all the rest. They made a new start, begot offspring, and left them capable of surviving in a new land.

Grandma, grandpa — here I am.

That afternoon, I rolled the dice one last time in search of Patrick Flood. A jeweler, a pub owner, and my old oracle all said that a little hamlet not far out of New Ross was a Flood town. I took a guess, thinking that at the turn of the century it was a good chance that Patrick lived within walking distance of Bridie. Most folks lived and died within five miles of their birthplace — that's why strangers were objects of such curiosity, interest, romance, and suspicion.

The little town is called The Rowers. A quiet crossroads with an air of old landed money combined with newer houses. I toured the Catholic church in the fading daylight and knelt to pray. Knocking on the rectory door brought me the pastor, everything one would want an Irish priest to be — all in black, white-haired, hearty. He instantly invited me in, and checked the parish database. He found no Floods.

He offered me tea. We sat and sipped and threw the same church-chat around that clergy always have and probably always will as long as the organized religious project endures. He spoke candidly of doing ministry in an increasingly prosperous and secular Ireland. He sighed and talked of empty seminaries and convents, young men and women choosing prosperous careers over the sacrifice involved in "a vocation." We spoke of the emerging scandals rocking the Roman church world-wide. He shook his head. "It was bound to happen. Ireland is becoming part of the larger world, no longer a refuge. We do need the money and the young need the jobs. But I do hope we don't lose our soul, what it is to be Irish."

I stood in the parish cemetery, watching the sun set through a tormented, harshly beautiful field of clouds over low hills. A cold wind through the graves told me that my search for Patrick Flood was over for now. He remains an enigma, a vanished man both in family story as well as here in the land of his birth. But he hadn't disappeared. He lived on in the breast of a lovely woman who died inside the day he died of the TB. He lived in the wonder and loneliness and longing of his daughter. He lives in my hunger to know how deeply Ireland's soil is worked into my fingers, how deep runs the sadness and the magic and the pride. And in three children, one named for his beloved, splendid and graceful and long-limbed, red-haired and a flowing flame on the soccer pitch. And in the saint whose name they both bear, lover of homes and hearths, keeper of hearts forever.

chapter 18

the whorl

I LIKED SUE and her husband and their comfy B&B very much, and felt like I was leaving Auntie Susie's house as I drove out of New Ross to take the twisting road north, to Castledermot and Moone, on the way to Kildare.

I had bought a cassette tape of all-that-Enya-ever-sung and played it until it grew hot to the touch. Then the radio, which played U2's "Beautiful Day" three times per hour. At that point I decided the humid rental car had no more room for both me and contemporary Celtic music. The rain and the wiper-slaps gave me all the music I wanted and needed as I drove and brooded. The shades of green kept finding more variations, and splatters of rain alternated with brief bursts of sun.

Castledermot is a significant-sized town with a large pub and no sign that I found to point out their legendary high crosses. Asking around the pub did not reveal many people who had much knowledge about high crosses, although the barkeep said that there were a "couple of stone crosses" in the cemetery.

Cemetery indeed — at its center was a medieval stone church managed as usual by the Church of Ireland. It was locked. A round tower — I am not enough of an archaeologist to tell if it was "period," a re-build, or a romantic later addition. And there were gravestones ranging from last week to last millennium, in neat and orderly rows. And among the graves were two intricate stone high crosses.

I walked round the crosses each in turn, circumambulating them, leaning forward to kiss them after stealing quick, guilty looks around the grounds to see who would think the Yank perverse to be intimate with the crosses. Fitful showers enforced breaks during which I leaned against the

130

church wall out of the rain and thoughtfully gazed at the crosses in their peaceful green setting. The Castledermot crosses are "Scripture crosses," covered with panels depicting biblical scenes with great intricacy, most of the figures bearing an unmistakably Celtic stamp with large heads and huge, spiritually eloquent eyes. Anyone with some knowledge of the Bible can puzzle out all or most of the scenes. Doing so is part of the fun of the crosses. Because venerable as they are, I am convinced that the crosses were meant to be enjoyed. Today they are a solemn and hoary gray, but many folks believe that they were originally painted, the figures given exuberant colors as arresting and forthright as any folk art.

The Three Young Men in the Babylonian furnace, Daniel in the lion's den — these images are frequent, almost ubiquitous, on the high crosses, and suggest that the monks were deeply conscious of martyrdom and the price that might be exacted for courageous faith. With Norse raiders on the rivers, swift in their long-ships and quick with their axes, such faith may be called upon suddenly and such a death easily had. And the one non-biblical scene that is also almost always found on the carved crosses is St. Antony meeting St. Paul the Hermit in the desert. Antony, one of the earliest and archetypal of the desert monks, came forth out of solitude to find soul-friendship and communion with Paul, one still more venerable than he. Here lies the mystery of the journey through solitude to communion, the pilgrimage each monk and in fact each one of us is called upon to walk.

I left the holy ground of Castledermot and drove north toward Moone.

On the way, I pulled over and stopped at a place that reeked of medieval hostelry. The Moone High Cross Inn is delightfully aged and loved and consists of a pub with lodging rooms upstairs and down. I so wish I had taken a room at the Moone High Cross Inn. If I ever return, I intend to rectify my mistake.

The jovial man at the bar, who thought my choice of tea over a pint showed poor judgment, sold me a densely written pamphlet showing the way to the Moone High Cross, with all of its known history and lots about high crosses in general. Armed with this authoritative bundle of photocopy, I sallied forth. No more than three minutes' drive took me to the Moone High Cross.

The cross lives today within the ruins of a monastery church tucked into overgrown woods off of a local farming road. The open-roofed ruins now serve as the shrine of the cross.

The Moone Cross is tall, very tall, a slender spire with ringed cruciform head shooting upwards from an elongated pyramidal base. The base itself teems with carved Celtic figures suggesting a gathered crowd of witnesses. Story panels alternate with powerful vital Celtic whorls and knots all over the cross, bursting with the primeval vitality that Celtic writers sometimes call *neart*, the vital force springing from the heart of God and partaking of the divine energy. The side of the cross-head facing the altar-side wall of the ancient church bears a Celtic-style crucified Christ in glory. But on the opposite side of the cross-head is carved a single powerful whorl, ceaselessly rotating and surging without moving a flake of the old gray stone. Like the Grail hidden in a forgotten trove, the cross burns silently, heedless of its abandoned setting.

I stood and struggled for breath, caught beneath the inexorable yet gentle gaze of that whirling eye. I felt beneath the surface of my skin a heat in spite of the chill and damp. The heat did not emanate from me but from the cross. I felt that if I stayed too long in its presence I would be burned.

My steps slow, almost dragging, I came closer. I reached out a trembling hand, feeling foolish that I expected the cross to be blisteringly hot to the touch. Cool, enduring my hand, the rough gray stone invited me. Slowly I stepped around clockwise, touching, tracing the powerful whorls and knots, leaning over to kiss, gingerly exploring the carved figures. The Three Young Men in the furnace, Daniel and his lions, and Antony and Paul sharing bread in the desert. Fire and claws, desert and bread.

May the holy Cross be my light, I prayed silently.

Even now in dreams, I step through the muddy threshold of those ruins and gasp as the cross, sapling-slender, shoots up from the ground before me. I awake with the vague but certain knowledge that I have been there again. I wrote at the time, "I feel as if the crosses' shadows have fallen on my heart. There they have made a permanent impress, a place for themselves and for the Crucified One."

Speechless within and without, I drove slowly for Kildare.

chapter 19

the well

I DON'T REMEMBER MUCH about the road from Moone to Kildare. Perhaps the dynamic whorl of the Moone Cross was spinning in my brain as well as in my soul. There was rain and gloom. The road was well-paved. I paid it no mind otherwise. I was longing for Kildare the way I would long for home when I was a tired, distressed school-kid.

The guidebook warned about the N-7 road cutting through Kildare. An endless stream of east-west traffic barrels through the heart of town. I was caught up in the torrent of grumbling trucks shouldering the weight of the economic Celtic Tiger, carrying whatever it is the Irish buy or the Irish sell and that the Irish cannot live without. At the traffic light, the hulking trucks barely concealed their impatience with yet another tourist proud of driving his rental car on the wrong side of the road. I entered the intersection and, pausing to turn, locked eyes with a graceful statue poised at the intersection. It was Herself, it was Brigid. She gazed patiently at the passing traffic, appearing to try to pray it into some semblance of calm.

I turned in front of her and the traffic whirled me away. I craned my neck painfully, reluctant to leave her statue behind. I felt as if I had failed to stop for the one familiar face in a crowd.

But I was immersed in twenty-first-century Kildare, and I found that the street map I possessed gave only hints and nudges toward any sense of my destination. But several right turns and a testy process of elimination got me to a B&B that was willing to take in off-season guests.

I used the "one-armed bandit" in the hallway to call Sister Mary, my local contact, who agreed with heartening enthusiasm to meet the next day. Her directions were detailed but oddly obscure, so I hung up with a shrug. Tired but hungry, I aimed the car back at the throbbing center of Kildare.

I passed the statue of Herself again and parked the car in a crowded lot outside of a cluster of brightly lit, busy-looking joints. The first one I entered was elbow-to-elbow with jolly Hibernian drunks, cheering with lusty glee a hurling match on TV. Not feeling lusty nor yet drunken, I moved on to a restaurant. I was seated by an elegant young woman, whose good manners I put to the test when I saw the prices on the menu and asked her where I might get something like pub grub instead. "Ah, that would be the pub, then," she said without obvious irony. She pointed through an open doorway, and I found myself in the world of bar and stools and tables and taps that was the usual end of my Irish days. Food and a pint and a soccer match on the pub TV got me through the evening, and I slept deeply that night.

The next morning was, I noted in my journal, "clear and cold." The cold gave me a sense of urgent immediacy — time and my stay were fading with the season, and so the time to seek and to ask was now.

What I planned to ask of the saint at her sacred well I also wrote down: what is my call? As priest, as husband, as father, as a man?

Now, some years after my solitary wanderings, I find myself smiling as I read my eager credulity approaching the shrines and stones of the saints. My faith has acquired a kind of reserve about its demands. Mustn't stretch God too far, you know, ask too much, hope for too much. But as I write this, I blush and realize that my faith has been watered down by fear of disappointment, the fear that I might discover that there really isn't anyone listening when I pray. I know now that one of the gifts of pilgrimage is that of immediacy and vulnerability, traveling at the mercy of God and of the hospitality of strangers, putting aside halting faith and allowing wonder and a wild hope to emerge. I hoped to meet Brigid that clear, cold Kildare day, and wrapped in that fragility and vulnerability I sallied forth, in ragged tweed and too-small cap and shoes that hurt.

I parked again in the chaotic center of Kildare town, the growling trucks now joined by the bustle of what turned out to be Thursday market day. I liked the look and feel of the stalls and people, and I

watched them while I stood outside of the downtown bank. My stock of
pence and pounds was low, and it was time to make exchange.

An old man asked, "Ye from Australia?" No, America. A pilgrim. He
looked at me keenly, and gave the smallest tilt of the head to where
Brigid's statue stood still attempting to calm the traffic. "Aye. This is a
holy city."

Pounds in hand, I wandered the market, and bought a shoulder-bag
from a man. The man asked, "Ye from Canada?" No, America. "Holiday?" Pilgrim. His face lit up. He had a Brigid's Cross, he did. If he'd
known I was coming, he'd have brought it for me. A man comes sometimes, sells them for a pound, for charity. "God bless you now," he said
as I walked away.

I stopped at a dignified-looking Catholic church, expecting to find a
small shrine or at least a stained-glass window of Brigid, but her absence
inside was conspicuous. The interior was baroque, well done if gaudy
and extremely ornate, a prayerful space nonetheless. I knelt, grateful for
holy ground on which to press my knees, and yet I felt lost, as if I had
gotten off a flight only to find no one to greet me at the gate. I remembered the diatribes I had read by right-wing Catholic clergy in the Irish
press against "Celtic spirituality," a "made-up commodity" composed of
"wishful thinking and barely baptized New Age paganism." Was I spend-
ing time and money wandering a chilly autumn Ireland chasing my own
ghosts and fantasies? I heavily dragged myself and the question both out
into the fitful daylight.

The gate of Brigid's Cathedral, with its round tower and fire-pit site,
was locked tight. A small sign suspended on the gate implied it was open
sometimes in season and only whimsically in the off.

I went in search of Sister Mary.

I washed up finally in the parking lot of a vast and ominous-looking
convent, a fit sight for a gothic murder story. I stared up at the row
of identical windows and gables and my heart plummeted through my
shoes to strike the parking lot tar. I envisioned Sister Mary as a forbidding
creature swathed in black, stern gray eyes peering through steel-rimmed
spectacles, as ready to grill me on the Catechism and to say cutting
things about Protestants as she would be to offer any solace.

A cry of "halloo" interrupted my bleak reverie.

A small, furiously energetic woman was toiling across the lot as if it were an uphill slope. She strode and grinned her way up to me with that kind of Irish Catholic panache that says grace may be free but you've got to work like hell at it, me boyo, so get on with it, we all do. Long live Pelagius, I thought to myself, as I asked my doughty Hibernian angel if Sister Mary were inside.

"Ah no, not a'tall, she lives the other side of town, and I'll tell you how to find her. Just saw her myself, I did, driving about the town. You just . . . no wait. Well . . . best I take you over there myself."

Pleased not to receive another set of hieroglyphic directions, I climbed into the rental and plunged after her across the raging river of N-7 traffic.

We pulled up, not at another Victorian rock-pile of a convent, but in a very suburban-looking cul-de-sac with modern-looking houses. "Sister Pelagius" motioned to one of the doorways. "There they are, the Brigids, there's their symbol, the flame you see, that's them, but Sister Mary doesn't seem to be about, but now there's her car, there she comes, she's often late, so much to do the poor love, bye now Father, bye Sister Mary." Waving vigorously in our general direction, the energetic woman of God disappeared into her car and rushed off. That is, if she was ever really there.

Sister Mary turned out to be a small, serene woman, dark-haired and young in soul. She greeted me graciously and kindly, treating me as if I were her most important and planned thing to do that day. She ushered me into the house that is the Kildare residence of the Sisters of St. Brigid, "revived," she said, "NOT founded, but restored" in the nineteenth century. We went to a long, cheery room, the "Brigid Room" she called it. She brought the inevitable but very welcome tea, and we talked and talked.

Some people have the gift of making one feel that one's soul has met theirs. It's a gift in a lonely world, where so many go about in involuntary solitude and isolation. Sister Mary was an oasis of listening and understanding, and as she spoke I felt I understood her as well.

She told me of the mission of the Brigids: to revive the spirit of Brigid through a healing and ecumenical ministry, to greet pilgrims and love the earth and re-light Brigid's fire of Gospel light and hope in a broken world. She told me that they were only two, herself and a companion, there in Brigid's city, but that their circle of affiliation, "Solas Bridhe," was ever-growing. She told me of her dream of building desert cells, solitary retreat cells, there in Kildare for pilgrims. She told me of both her fiery vision and of her tiredness. To carry a great vision, I learned, is as wearying as any other load.

I told her of my hopes and my struggles with my ministry and with the parish, and how we sought both healing and a vision. I told her something of my family and their wounds. She closed her eyes and her whole body smiled with gratitude when I told her how the vendor had gotten excited when I told him I was a pilgrim, and how the old man had said that Kildare was "a holy city."

The phone rang, she left the room, and I sat and looked about.

In the corner was a sort of tumulus, I don't know how else to describe it. It was composed of draped cloth over some object which made the whole suggest a mountain. Sacred objects of various sorts decorated the miniature peak. In the center was lit a tall, clear glass votive candle.

The flame drew me, and I was out of my chair without my realizing I was in motion. I approached the place and knelt to pray in silence.

Sister Mary re-entered the room and stopped, smiling. "I'm sorry that we were interrupted, but I see you've been enjoying your time." She explained that the flame was actually Brigid's Fire, preserved since it was rekindled in the early '90s at a justice and peace conference in Kildare. Brigid's Fire, the old Druidic fire in the sacred oak grove that bold Brigid had found and had reconsecrated to the Trinity, the fire which she and her nuns had tended for a millennium until impious feet stamped it out in the sixteenth century.

The tiny flame danced, as if chuckling. I had found Brigid.

Mary had brought reeds from her own garden. As we talked on, she wove a large Brigid's cross. She blessed me with it and gave it me. "I wove your and your parish's intentions into this cross."

So I left, blessed by the present Abbess of Kildare. I had found Brigid, but had still to pose my question to her.

Mary had given me a small booklet, which prescribes a pattern through Kildare. The end is Brigid's Well.

I parked the car at the parish church of St. Brigid, the "other" Roman Catholic church in town. Here, from the main door handles shaped like outstretched feminine hands, to the stone altar with the blocks cunningly arranged to form a Brigid's Cross, there was enough Brigid even for me. A side shrine was donated, as a plaque said, by the Anglicans to the people of St. Brigid's Parish. Trust Brigid to bring the Protestants and the Catholics together.

I left the church to find the streets alive with local schoolchildren, their prim uniforms a contrast to the fireworks they were gleefully setting off. I have no clue as to whether the day was some sort of school holiday, or if recess in Kildare is usually accompanied by explosions. A rocket skittered past my feet as some of the kids shouted something. I waved vaguely, feeling as if I was gazing at them from a great distance of time as well as of place.

Only for a moment did I wonder if I should walk or drive from the church to the Well. Pilgrimage is for walking. I swung my pack on my back and strode off down the road out of Kildare Town.

The grass soon turned rich and green, a soft and delectable carpet lying in luxurious folds on both sides of the road. Kildare is horse country, the location of the National Stud. Brigid was reputed to love horses. Some say that the legend of Brigid became entangled with a horse-goddess cult. Whatever the truth of it, horses still reign in Kildare's fields. I shook my head to clear it of all the random associations the words "National Stud" gave rise to and walked on.

On the left rose a gray square-topped stone ruin. The Black Abbey, said the booklet. It is the ruins of a "caravansary" or fortified monastery of the Knights Hospitallers of St. John, one of the medieval military orders of monks charged with guarding Jerusalem pilgrims and making war upon the "infidel." The Knights have a checkered history, but when I was younger I had thrilled to the heroic account of the Knights' defense of Malta in the sixteenth century against a vastly superior Turkish force. I stood on the road and saluted the old Knights, and asked them for a warrior's heart.

Past the Black Abbey and on the same side of the road is the first of the two wells of Brigid. This one was walled-in, but was a peaceful spot at which to stop. I did not sense any strong presence there, at least not for me. I sat and prayed and somehow got a sense that this well was one frequented by young people, young lovers.

The road to the main Well led to the right, perpendicular to the road leading out of Kildare.

I walked it slowly. As I did, a sense of solitude engulfed me. But in the heart of the solitude, amidst hearing my feet scrunch on the gravel, I felt the press of others around me. A multitude, whom I could not see, but they were there, walking, even jostling a bit. I was swept along with them, up the simple path from the road that was marked "Brigid's Well."

Now, faith and consciously evoked archetypes and powerful myths can be a potent brew. Coming to Brigid's Well was the culmination of a lifelong journey that began when my mother first wove the stories of sorrow and longing and loss that was her family's pilgrimage, and when she first breathed the name "Brigid" into my ear. This journey had continued when I came to serve as priest of an urban church perched on a highway of broken humanity, and Brigid's icon and name appeared in the hall where food is served to the poor.

As for what happened next, all I can do is tell the tale.

The Well is reached by crossing a small wooden footbridge spanning a lively stream. The pilgrim guidebook invites a pause on the bridge to recite the Rosary. I did so. The beads slipped through my fingers and I thought of all the hands and all the beads that had moved here before, tendrils of prayers, worn threads of faith.

Over the bridge, I found that the stream flowed past a Roman-style Marian shrine, which to me looked anachronistic and excessive in this older Celtic setting. Water and wood and grass and stone are all the ornaments really needed.

Past this shrine, the stream issues forth from a pair of stone projections that are so breast-like that I was jolted by their matter-of-fact symbolism. Brigid, Mary of the Gael, Foster-mother of Christ . . . I paused at the place where the waters flow ceaselessly from the stone breasts, and felt with humble gratitude the ceaseless flow of grace the motherly love of God.

Before me at last, at the end of a small lawn, was the Well.

The distance between it and where I stood was measured out by small rough stones, not even knee-high. The guidebook suggested approaching the Well slowly, prayerfully, pausing at each stone to pray. For peace . . . for justice . . . for the poor . . . for healing. . . .

At last, having trouble getting my breath, I was before the Well.

It is enclosed by a low stone wall, again not even knee-high. The wall is shaped simply, the sweep of stones suggesting that it embraces those who approach.

I stared down into the waters — dark but clear, speckled with tiny green seeds of some sort fallen from the tree which almost overhangs the Well. I knew in that moment that here was one of the *omphalos*, one of the navels of the earth, a place which descends to the Center.

I stood hurriedly and circumambulated the Well three times in the ancient way, reciting the prayers suggested. As I did so, I noted that the branches of the nearby tree was festooned with cloth strips, *clooties*, each bearing a prayer — and other objects, enigmatic but plaintive in what they beseeched of God and the Saint. Rosaries, hair scrunchies, letters, eyeglasses, a driver's license. . . .

The circles complete, I knelt before the Well and laid open before it the book of petitions written by my parishioners. I knelt upright and began to pray. "It's been a long time. . . . "

That is as far as I got. My body began to be wracked with sobs so deep and raw they would have frightened me, save that I knew that of all places on earth where it was safe for me to cry, to release the tears I had long held inside, it was here. It was here, where tear upon unnumbered tear had been shed, misery and exile had found a home, the poor had found their God and their Mother's compassionate ear.

I gasped and sobbed, body shaking. The only words I could hear from my own mouth that made any sense were "Mother" and "Oh God."

Into the Well I poured everything I carried — my grandparent's rejection and their paupers' death in a strange land's ghetto, my mother's and family's alienation, my father's bitter sojourn seeking peace, my own loneliness, the pain I brought and the pain I caused, my wife's struggle far from her family and her family's pain, my children trying to make sense of their own lives, my parish's longing and floundering and questions and grief... everything. I poured and poured, like a loaded wheelbarrow tilted and held until everything slithers out.

And the Well took it all, took it without a ripple to disturb its surface, room within for a thousand such burdens and more, took it all until my body shuddered to stillness, my tears ceased, and there was nothing inside me but emptiness. I stayed suspended, somehow still existing even though all that had been inside, that had filled me and given shape to me like stuffing inside a rag doll, was gone.

And then from the Well there flowed green fire and water, laving me, flowing over and within me, washing and filling and cleansing all at once. I gasped and stayed still, inundated and immersed.

And all ceased and was still, and I was kneeling on rough stone on the edge of an old well on a cold autumn day in Ireland, gazing down into still water. I reached down, hand nerveless and without strength, and dipped some of the cold, green-smelling water and laved my face, my arms, touched my lips.

A clean, cold breeze sprang up from the nearby green field. It snatched playfully at the book of petitions and whipped it open. I glanced down at the page and saw written there, in the hand of a grieving widow, "The strength to go on."

The road was long back to Kildare. The town rimmed the horizon with a medieval look, church spires the highest points. A young man walked along the road toward me. He caught my eye and smiled as if he knew me. "Cheers," he said.

chapter 20

to Return and
tell the tale

I DID NOT FULLY realize it then, but Kildare and its healing well and gentle, fire-bearing saint was the end of my journey. I had days to go still in Ireland, but in Kildare my burden had been lifted and my pilgrim vow, I believe, redeemed. I was ill at ease for the balance of my time in Ireland, for which I am sorry but could not fake or lie about then or now. In my mind's eye there was a labyrinth path that I was following, but the turn had been made and it was leading back out from the center and toward home.

I drove from Kildare to a residence called Bellinter House in the midst of County Meath. By day I ventured forth. I drove to Newgrange, site of some of the ancient mounds already old when the Celtic invaders arrived. The entrance to the chief and most famous mound, actually a beautifully designed vast earth and stone structure, is guarded by massive loaf-shaped boulders covered with powerful carved knots and whorls. Inside is a small chamber that is dark save for the single slender shaft of sunlight that enters on the morning of the winter solstice. I stood and marveled — how they reverenced the light! And how we take the light for granted, in spite of our belief that we are the ones who are "advanced."

And I found the "jewel in the crown," the high crosses of Monasterboise.

The ruins are found off a quiet road. Inside the gates is found the usual crowded welter of graves as at every former Celtic monastic site. The round tower is impressive. But the great high crosses there are among the most intricately carved and best renowned in all Ireland. They are truly "Scripture crosses," Bibles in stone. I did appreciate, though, as I stood and peered in the failing light of day, that at the bottom of one of the crosses is carved two guys, sitting cross-legged opposite one another, each gripping the other's beard and for all eternity fighting a facial hair tug-of-war. God bless the nameless carver, I thought grinning; he didn't want anyone to get too serious or too bored, least of all himself.

I left Bellinter House and met my brother Rick at Dublin Airport.

Of all my five brothers, Rick and I have gone the furthest physically from New York and the rest of the family. At that time living in London, he only had to hop a British Midlands flight over to Dublin to meet up with his kid brother in Ireland.

I took him to Glendalough. We ate and drank in the crowded pub in Laragh, walked the monastery grounds and talked. It was good and healing to walk together in a place that our ancestors may have come to in pilgrimage. Later that night, I showed Rick the notes I had taken from the afternoon I spent in the rectory parlor in New Ross, all I could find of Bridie and the Morrisseys. He sat with the handwritten papers in hand and mused, "A life, a whole life, and nothing left but bits of paper." But by now you may guess that pensive moroseness runs in my family.

I put Rick on his plane back to Blighty and headed for Dublin.

I found I did not have the heart for things that I would love to do some other time — the James Joyce pub crawl, the Guinness brewery tour. I did make my way down to the Temple Bar district, and drank a pint singing along with a "trad" combo that had a penchant for the old rock band America. I visited Christ Church Cathedral and found the tomb of William LeClare, the Norman "Strongbow" who came ashore and built his abbey at New Ross. I looked down at his recumbent marble image atop his tomb, and thought of his wife's sarcophagus abandoned and open to the rain in New Ross churchyard. Stooping, I whispered to Strongbow, "Man, are you in trouble when she catches up with *you*."

I found my way to the National Museum and saw wonders: Saint Patrick's bell in its ornate case, and the Ardagh Chalice, a wide and deep vessel with beautiful enameled designs without and within. Some wishful romantics thought it was a candidate for being the actual Holy Grail. In the Viking section, in a floor-level glass case lay the skeleton of a Viking warrior. I gazed in awe at the huge skeletal frame, broad shoulders, massive skull with huge jaws, immense sword held in his bony hands, and shuddered. Written records from the Viking era in Ireland are full of lurid tales of Norse brutality and the terror they spread, describing them as huge pagan demons, blond giants filled with terrible rage. I had sometimes put down many of the tales to angry medieval "spin," outraged propaganda, and that back then a man 5'9" would be called tall. Now I looked down at the bones of one of those of whom the monks prayed, "Deliver us, O Lord, from the fury of the Northmen." I felt a sickening wrench in my gut, a kind of atavistic ancestral fear. I looked in the great gaping eye sockets and whispered, "Sorry for the indignity of the display case, soldier. I'd bury you if I could. But for the record, I'm glad you're dead and not standing in front of me, you big bastard."

And I saw the great treasure of the Western World.

The Book of Kells is housed with other ancient monastic manuscripts at Trinity College, Dublin. It is thought by some today that the Book, an illuminated manuscript of the Gospels, was created largely on Iona and only taken away to Kells for safekeeping. The Vikings got hold of it once on a raid, but the monks followed and found the manuscript in a bog. The Norse had torn off the gold and jeweled cover and gone away satisfied, and the monks, recovering the manuscript, were satisfied as well.

In the margin of another monastic manuscript was found a poem, written by the monk-scribe about himself and his pet:

> I and Pangur Ban my cat,
> Tis a like task we are at
> Hunting mice is his delight
> Hunting words I toil all night. . . .

Over the doorway I saw inscribed, in a Celtic uncial flourish, "I and Pangur Ban my cat. . . ."

Inside was a well-done exhibit on the history and creation of the Irish manuscripts. The exhibit ended at a large doorway, over which was inscribed the last line of the Pangur poem, "And I bring darkness into light."

In a round space inside, under heavy glass in a soft pool of light, lay the Book of Kells, open to the Gospel of John. The colors glowed and pulsed with their own inner light. I moved closer, breathless, then back, then forward again and again. I could not get enough of the book's beauty, its gentle, penetrating light.

I sidled up to one of the watchful guards and asked, "Do you ever get used to being in the same room with these books?"

She stared, then looked me in the eyes and smiled slowly, knowingly. "Never."

I should be so blessed as to so bring darkness into light.

As I flew out of Dublin, I was torn. I was eager to be home and with my family, yet reluctant to leave the soil that I felt moistened with my ancestral blood, the stones where those whose faith and ministry gave birth to my own had lived and worked and died. I wondered if I would ever return. I wonder still.

The U.S.-bound plane muscled itself into the air, tearing its wheels and my soul free of Europe.

I was surprised to find myself moved by the sight of U.S. flags and uniforms. It is good to have a country, and one's country, with all her checkered history and dubious policies, is always one's own. For all that, I winced silently at the loud and brassy language and the quarrelsome and whiny conversations I overheard. I wanted to take aside at random any person I caught complaining and tell them quietly how good they had it — to have a country, to feel reasonably safe, to be warm and clothed and as secure as any of us can feel.

Portland looked wonderfully familiar. I teared up at the sight of my beautiful, precious family. I could not stop touching them, assuring myself that they were real. My clothes hung off me, for in spite of the pub grub and the daily pint or two I had lost weight in Ireland. The walking? I recommend the pub and walking diet and wish I were on it now.

And so I picked up the threads of my life, all in a bundle really. All asked me in some measure, "How was it?" At first, I found myself at a loss for words. Is there any way that one can describe walking in the trail of the dead, ancient echoes of passionate faith, a land which is and is not one's home, and not babble like a fool? Or question one's own sanity?

Slowly, haltingly, I began to tell pilgrim tales. To individuals, in brew-pubs where the feel of the cool pint glass took me easily back to other pubs, other places, within easy journeys of ancient crosses and silent ruins. To groups — the gracious Episcopal Churchwomen's group, who assured me that they love my storytelling. To a small group of men from the parish: we met in the basement of the local Trappist abbey and I spread out the map of Iona, and all day we spoke of pilgrimage, journey, initiation, and becoming a man of Christ, a peaceful warrior of the Gospel. Often I felt ill at ease, uprooted, and detached from my own culture as I did when I returned from the Philippines. Often I felt foolish, as if I had taken an expensive middle-class vacation prettified with elite spirituality. How would this connect with anyone else's life?

In 2001 I took the remainder of my sabbatical. I began to write. I walked into a tae kwon do class and watched, then went home and dared my son to join with me. Daughter Bridget piped up, "Me too!" and now it's been five years and all three of us have our black belts and Jake is going for second degree. The chief instructor, Master Cynthia Brown, I count as a kind of soul-friend and a vital person in our family life. From tae kwon do I have learned enough to fill another book. Suffice it to say that I think the lesson that Columba taught his monks — that one can be a peaceful warrior of God — I learned in the sweat of exercise halls and tournaments. And tae kwon do taught me of communities of intention: people can rise to the challenge of a difficult discipline and grow together, supporting each other through difficulty and sacrifice, working toward a noble goal. I watched and wondered how I could help form a church that built deep supportive bonds while challenging one another to grow into a disciplined life in Christ.

Thoughts like these continued to ferment as the weeks and months went on.

I think an "authentically Celtic" process consists of stories and conversations, speaking and listening, and allowing time for this to happen and not leaping to "the plan." I listened to the spiritual hungers extant in our parish. Some longed for a consecrated life, a life focused on seeking

God. Others sought a community of faith and study even amidst their family demands. Others sought meaningful service to the poor who flock around the church. The conversations grew and connected.

All seemed to cry out for making a re-imagined Celtic Christian vision live again.

A great deal of talk and writing goes into diagnosing why many ways of "being church" and "doing church" either don't work anymore, or even if they work the result looks and feels more like American culture than it does the radical values of the Gospel. Ever since Constantine made Christianity the official "imperial faith," Christians have been trying to push the camel of power and wealth through the slender needle's eye of the vision of Jesus. What is going on these days is an older "empire" model of Christianity, the traditional "mainline," has given up center stage to the new imperial Christianity, which some of my friends call the "dominant evangelical paradigm." Why each era thinks they can do better than the Holy Roman Empire is a mystery beyond me.

But the Celtic Christians founded vibrant communities of seekers and pilgrims, scholars and poets and mystics, dynamic and restless, while Rome fell and came close to taking the Roman church with it. Pilgrimage, prayer, a mystic's eye, dynamic community, scholarship, a gift for seeing God everywhere in the world . . . all this says that the Spirit of God is not bound to any structure or polity and can bring about new vibrant life even when it seems that everything, even sacred things, are winding down to death.

Many churches these days are in some measure implicitly Celtic. Most churches possess a membership not determined by who lives nearby so much as who makes the journey in to worship and make common life with this particular community. And those who seek community in Christ are not seeking to fulfill any social and civic obligation. They are coming to seek God. We are pilgrims. Denominational infighting is more and more ridiculous in the face of a hurting and hungry world, self-referential and unattractive. Who wants to buy into such a thing? And those who come as seekers seek a whole life, to experience themselves as gifted and graced and as people who may pray and rejoice and serve. None of this is uniquely Celtic. But it is distinctly Celtic, and recapturing the Celtic tradition and making it live puts us in company with tradition in its best sense, tradition as wise life lived wisely by brave, ragged pilgrim souls whose very bones are now dust and whose homes are worn stones lying in the grass, but whose lives shine on.

What if, I wondered, we began to reconceive the parish church as a Celtic-patterned monastery? What if the focus of the community was not maintenance, but mission and nurturing the passion of pilgrims? What if we welcomed and honored pilgrims and saw ourselves as living on pilgrimage? What if, like the traditional Celtic communities which included people of many states of life, there were various opportunities to live a committed and passionate path within the parish "bounds," the modern invisible *vallum*? What if we broke through the walls separating church from neighborhood, and from other churches? What if we were to truly be a place where the poor and the most abused could find refuge? What if the future flowed from the gifts of our members, the gifts of which God is so lavish in giving, and we followed those gifts and let those gifts determine our plan?

People from outside the parish kindled at this forming vision and contributed their own passion and dreams. One early gift of this has been losing the sense of competing for the "sheep." People can be called to one congregation or another, or called to worship in one place but exercise a ministry in another.

I sat down and wrote what had been fermenting on some level of my brain and drinking deeply of all the conversations we all had shared. What came out is what some these days like to call a Big Hairy Audacious Goal. The Columba Center: not a program, nor yet a nonprofit agency, but rather a vision that transforms parish community and makes its borders porous. The original vision, already changed and still a work in progress, is found in one of the appendices.

I envisioned a community founded on a deep experience of God the Trinity, which would welcome all yet offer challenge and support for those who hungered for a deeper life in Christ. I envisioned writing a Rule of Life, perhaps more than one, which would represent a new adaptation of monastic life. The poor and the marginalized were to be welcomed and care offered, remembering the loss of dignity that can take place for the poor even amidst kind people of good intentions. And we were to break down barriers between our church and other churches, between us and the neighborhood, between us and any of good will who share our vision of spiritual seeking and of service and of community-building, of the arts and of creativity.

I still at times worry that all this is my private conceit, my midlife crisis hobby. But at my age I am less and less inclined to squander my time in "playing the church game" to the satisfaction of those few who need a frozen and limited version of the church as polite social institution and familiar purveyor of comfort. I want to live as a pilgrim myself, to seek and to serve and to immerse myself in the depths of the ever-fascinating mystery of God.

The question was: will this vision make sense to anyone else?

Some scratched their heads and asked, "What does it mean?" "So what do we *do?*" A few told me they "weren't into the Celtic thing" or were waiting for the "Celtic craze" to fade away just like other church trends they had experienced. One early supporter, himself a professed member of an Episcopal monastic Order, said prophetically, "We will need to be open to how the Lord will increase or decrease us." And this has proven to be true. On the one hand, the Columba Center has not created a mass exodus from the parish. A few who found they don't connect with the vision have drifted into the peripheries or left altogether. On the other hand, the Columba Center has not been the cause of explosive numerical growth. But people have come, slowly but increasingly, drawn and kindled by the vision and saying that they have longed for just this sort of community, just this sort of life within the church.

In the spring of 2002 we announced a gathering of all those interested in the Columba Center vision. About fifty committed parish members came. I stood next to an imitation stone Celtic cross while I spoke and people asked questions. One participant said, "I thought you were announcing the creation of a social service agency. But instead you're inviting us on a voyage."

The vestry, the equivalent of the church board, discussed the vision over three meetings starting that spring. One vestryman was passionate: "When I read this I think, of course! This is what we should be doing and the only thing that we should be doing!" But consensus was not immediate. I unhooked myself from results as much as I could and quietly welcomed the conversations that came to me informally and via e-mail. One member told me, "I'm behind you. I just won't be out there next to you carrying a banner."

I sat back from the computer screen and opened my right hand. I felt there, for a fleeting moment, the rough wooden staff that Kevin had left for me leaning against that Glendalough tree. I had chosen to take it, after all. Don't pick up the staff, me boyo, unless you're ready to carry it about for real.

That August the vestry voted unanimously that the Columba Center vision was to be the "mission direction of the parish."

Such decisions often need to be re-owned. As I write we are in just such a process. Riches and fame have not been ours. But I'll tell you what has been ours: It's been frustrating fun. It's been costly honesty. It's been a lonely way to form and find community. It's led us to a larger and more hope-filled world. It's been a way to be alive. And it's been a way to make and participate in a future rooted in Christ.

chapter 21

BRIGID'S mantle,
RAHAB'S SISTERS

B RIGID OF KILDARE, it is told, never asked small. It's amazing that people in her time, especially the wealthy and the powerful, let her ask anything at all. Donald Trump, hearing her name on his intercom, would have left hastily by his office's back door.

Once, when Brigid had just established herself in Kildare, she and her sisters approached the local *ri*, the clan king who held the land thereabouts. She asked for land on which to expand her monastery as well as to work to raise food for her community and for the poor. Brigid's reputation preceded her, for the king laughed, wanting to play a version of the Celtic warrior-challenge with the famously bold Brigid and to out-match her in a battle of wits. "Very well," he said. "You may have land. You may have as much land as you can cover with your mantle." For Brigid wore a full cloak, probably cowled and possibly marked with a rope-cross on the back in the manner of the Desert Fathers and Mothers.

Brigid was game and accepted the offer. So she and her sisters set out her mantle on the ground, prayed, and began to pull the mantle out straight and taut. And they pulled and pulled. And much to the king's dismay and the reduction of his real estate, the mantle pulled and stretched until it lay over the whole of the rich green land now known as the Curragh, all about Kildare.

The only thing more risky than saying "yes" to Brigid, it seems, was saying "no" to Brigid, especially when she had generosity to the poor in mind.

This is another story of Brigid's Mantle, and how it has stretched and pulled until now it lays over an urban neighborhood in the East Side of Portland, Oregon, in the less-than-sunny Pacific Northwest.

The Irishness that my mother imparted to me she did so by stories. Through them I grew accustomed to the emotional geography of my own soul as well as that of dead relatives I had never met. I would meet them there, in that strange land born of the telling, when the teacups would rattle or the pungent citronella candles would sputter, late at night in the backyard.

But in and amongst the stories of Uncle John and Cousin Alfred-who-knew-Kevin-Barry were clues, breadcrumbs that left a trail that led into the mist. One of these crumbs was the name of Brigid, St. Brigid that is. My mother seemed to know little of her, other than that she was Irish, she was mysteriously great, and she had a role in the lives of the immigrant Irish. She *was* them, seemingly, their pride and their lost roots, and she protected them.

I learned little else in those days. A sulkily good little Catholic boy, I looked Brigid up in one of those ubiquitous little saints' lives books given to Catholic kids. Nothing there was much help. Brigid was there dressed like a severe high medieval-style nun, with those uncomfortable-looking swaddling cloths strapped to the chin like grave-bands around Jacob Marley's head. There was a single page of the usual resume bullets expected of a female saint in good standing — little miracle here, some act of impossibly patient goodness there. Her face bore the typical fatuous, rather stoned look of religious good taste and kindness, with a glowingly flawless complexion. I always figured that good skin was a requirement of sanctity (which left me out, especially in high school). I even wondered if it was religious ambition that led my mother to be such a faithful user of moisturizing cold cream.

Brigid receded into the half-remembered mist of my young years and the treacly Catholicism of my past. But Brigid, it seemed, was not content to stay where I'd left her. Years later, she came back.

Brigid came back as I learned the ebb and flow of the Celtic yearly cycle. As an assistant at a very busy, very suburban parish in St. Louis, I found my ministry fulfilling but a depth of my soul left untouched. I hungered for a way to make real the hard lessons of justice and liberation that I had imbibed in the Philippines and in urban Chicago. I longed also for the taste of a more visceral faith, one which comprehended the strange rhythms of creation and the turning year, one which regarded imagination and story and legend and the uncanny intuitive not with suspicion or derision, but as places where God may be met and Christ may transform.

I learned that it was the ancient Celtic Samhainn fire-feast that had been transformed into All Hallows Eve/All Saints/All Souls, where the living and the dead were intimate once more and healing through conversation with the Otherworld was possible. And so we celebrated All Hallows at Emmanuel with an oak fire and pumpkin-carving and storytelling in the autumn evening, and bagpipers then led us to the memorial garden where the prayers of the church were read.

And May was Beltane, the old spring fest whose revels were transformed by Patrick, some say, with the first Easter fire in old Eire, so that the old Celtic king-fire from which all hearth fires were lit became Christ's rising-fire, the Light that does not die.

And in the cold of Midwestern February 1, a hope of spring — ancient Imbolc, the seed-time and the lambing, Brigid's Day and promise of light and birth and hearth-warmth and new light. I wore the woven Brigid's Cross on the lapel of my rummage-sale Harris tweed and felt much better about the cold.

I had thought only a little of Brigid once I had started at Saints Peter and Paul. But she came nevertheless.

She came long before my pilgrimage, when my wife was in labor with Helen, our third-born. During the contractions, the fetal monitor began to tell a frightening tale — Helen's vital signs were fluctuating, heart rate dropping slowly but steadily, and my wife's blood pressure had begun to bounce as well. The young midwife looked worried, and the doctor on duty began to appear at the door with greater frequency. They began to speak softly but urgently of the possible need for an emergency C-section. My anxiety over Dina's health as well as the unborn baby washed over me like a cold, clinging tide.

I felt empty and ravaged as the doctor and midwife left the room. As my wife concentrated on her labor and I did what little even the most concerned husband can do, I prayed a desperate prayer. I prayed to Jesus Christ, who was himself empty and helpless, so that we might be full. And I remembered the old Irish birth-charm.

I rose and went to the door and opened it softly. Tears blurring my eyes, I spoke to the empty hall in a whisper. "Come Brigid, come foster-mother of Christ. Come to the bedside of this your daughter. Come with strong hand and healing touch. In the name of the One who is Three."

The midwife re-entered and took up her silent watch in the rocking chair. There was something inexpressibly timeless about the sight, the young Irish-descended knee-woman, rocking and keeping vigil. In the silence, it seemed that in that hospital chamber I could hear the stir and crackle of a gently burning fire.

And I, a man drowning in my fear, swore a desperate oath: "If you want to be part of the ministry of the parish, and of mine, and if you want us to take better care of the poor and lost on the street outside the church doors, then I'll see to it. Only save my child, save my wife."

A peace came over that room, the child unseen and the mother in labor and the young-old midwife rocking. The baby's vital signs steadied. And she was born that rainy November day less than an hour later.

Standing alone in the parking lot, relief making my knees weak, I remembered my promise to Brigid, to Herself. Living or dead, an Irishwoman never forgets. "Now I've done it," I thought.

Not long after that we renamed the Wednesday night meal program "Brigid's Table." Our deacon at that time found a lovely ikon of Brigid in an Orthodox bookstore. In it she stands before her Church of the Oak in Kildare, the round tower in the background, holding a staff, swathed in a lovely Celtic cloak. In her arm is cradled a parchment in which can be read her determination, according to record, to "save every miserable man." We installed her icon with a hanging lamp in the dining hall. And Brigid's Table the meal program is to this day. Something changed. The Wednesday night meal had always been a rich, good ministry. But a gentle presence, strong, that brings forth rich gifts from others, newness and a relationship of mutuality with our guests, who pray for us and teach us of God as we pray for them, now dwells at the heart of this ministry.

But she and God were not content.

Brigid came again when a young mother-to-be tearfully told me that an ultrasound showed that the unborn had a deformity that would require immediate surgery after birth. She asked for prayers. We stood before the Walsingham Marian shrine in the back of the church, and we prayed as I blessed her with a *caim*, the old Celtic prayer of encircling protection. And we lit a candle and invoked the Three and Brigid by name. "Foster-mother of Christ, knee-woman to all in labor, come and bless this daughter of yours, bless this child." And I re-made my oath, to reach out from the parish to those in need.

The next ultrasound showed clear, no deformities visible on the child. I tell you this: as I couldn't make this stuff up, or at least I wouldn't.

Another mother, with difficult pregnancies — we prayed, and invoked Brigid. The child was born whole and well.

I realized that was three, counting my own child. Frankly I felt hemmed in by it all, as if Brigid were beginning to send me bills with "past due" stamped on the front. One day, alone so as to avoid any more material for insanity hearings than I have already accumulated, I shook my fist at her icon. "And what'll you have then? What else can we do?"

Her candle sputtered briefly, impudently.

I spoke with my wife Dina, and with Mary Stilwell, a parishioner who was encouraging my pilgrimage, off and on about what more we were called to do. Mary allowed as how Brigid was drawing her mantle wider over Montavilla, and we simply needed to see what she was to cover. Dina reminded me of the women.

The women . . . 82nd Avenue and environs is heavy with prostitution activity. Our church parking lot has itself been the scene of tricks turned. I've watched the ceaseless trade, the endless walking, the women and young girls with cocky steps or weary feet or soulless, haunted faces, walking dead, the cars passing and passing and stopping, and wondered how in the world to reach out. Jesus was noted for his keeping company with prostitutes, telling the Pharisees that these despised women were entering the Kingdom before them. But they move as if swimming in fluid all their own, in a gulf, a tank far removed from the bourgeosie day-world of a middle-class priest and his appointments and his Sunday preparations. We spoke, a number of us at the parish, of the women and of what we could do. Churches are supposed to know and serve and reach out to their neighbors. They were, they are our neighbors.

All this wondering was part of the pack I hauled to Kildare and shoved into Herself's well. There came the answer, the green fire and water. A gift had been given. But in the paradoxical way of gifts of the Gospel, it would take work and risk to unwrap it.

Back at Saints Peter and Paul, life had resumed after stories had been told and pictures shared. And the women, as always, swam past the wooden walls and dusty windows of the church, restless as always in their urban aquarium.

One day, the tank was breached, and a brave survivor thrashed at our feet.

It was a Thursday morning, and the usual congregation of mostly retirement-aged ladies were preparing for their Bible study after Mass. I was upstairs doing God knows what. One of the ladies ascended the stairs and told me that there was a young woman downstairs. She had taken refuge in the church because "her boyfriend" had beaten her on the street. The Thursday ladies had let her in and, Brigid-bold, had locked the door in the man's face.

The full story of the chaos of what then ensued would take many a page to tell. Suffice it to say that the Portland police responded promptly, and we sat together with the woman as she told her story. She said that her mother had told her, "If you're in trouble and afraid, go to a church." As is so typical in battering, she was reluctant to press charges. She looked at me beseechingly. I put aside my usual nondirective ethos and told her, "You came here so you would be safe. Now I will tell you how to be safe. Make the complaint, swear the charges. Because whenever he hits you, he'll say later that he's sorry, that he'll be better, that he loves you, right? But each time he'll hit harder. And he'll never stop."

She pressed the charges. The walls seemed to suddenly ooze cops, blue shirts and t-shirts and bulging chests from Kevlar vests and holsters and conversations carried on with armpits. They pounced on the man in the parking lot and I watched with grim satisfaction as a powerful young cop put him up against a car. The police knew their business and, able for once to prosecute a battering case, took care of things. With the help of a competent young victims' advocate, they conducted the woman to a safe house.

Alone at last I stood in the empty church hall, the air still seeming to swim with blue shirts and guns and voices filled with their own authority. I looked up. There, above the doorway to the next hall, hung Brigid's cross, the woven reed cross that Sister Mary had made and given us in Kildare. I stared transfixed at the center diamond, the apex where the woven reeds meet to present what looks like an eye. As I stared, in my mind's eye it glowed gleefully, with fierce delight, green fire and water.

"And so, you called her in, did you? All your doing. And now what?"

The cross said nothing, nothing at least that I could hear. But the eye seemed to glow still as I locked up and left for the day.

When I told Mary, she said, "She's calling them in."

But how would she call them? And what to do when they came?

These questions began to be answered in a comfortable meeting room, by a quiet, articulate young priest looking for an altar and a call.

I was still serving on the Diocese's Commission on Ministry when Eleanor Applewhite-Terry, a transitional deacon, came and met with us. Eleanor had come from Connecticut, following her husband Bronson's pediatric residency at one of the city's hospitals. She was knocking about, functioning as a deacon and doing a little preaching, at Christ Church Lake Oswego as well as at other places.

When asked where she would most like to serve, Eleanor told of her time in Washington, D.C., working as staff in a residential home for women in addiction recovery. She spoke too of work in a parish in urban New Haven, Connecticut, which has its own abundant "mean streets" only blocks from the rarefied halls of Yale. She said she looked for "urban and gritty."

I sat forward in my chair. At the break, Shannon Leach, the rector of Lake Oswego, earned my lasting gratitude by bending over and whispering, "I saw how you looked at her and listened to her. If you want her at Saints Peter and Paul, then now's the time. Speak up, go after her."

When we reconvened, I spoke up and said that I had urban and gritty to spare, and she should come and see. Not long after, she did.

Again I would need another chapter to tell of the gift that Ellie has been to the parish and to myself, she who showed the parish what a called woman in Holy Orders can do. The parish loved Ellie and I hear no more muttering about "women priests." As I write, she and Bronson have returned to the Northeast with their adopted baby boy and I miss her and them like thunder in the mountains. But it is the women of 82nd Avenue who have benefited deeply from Ellie's time, for a ministry began with her and other women of the diocese, lay and ordained, through which Brigid calls her daughters to safe harbor.

For Ellie and Sara Fischer and Marla McGarry-Lawrence and Marilyn Brown and Chris Thurston and others began a work of outreach to women in prostitution that they dubbed "Rahab's Sisters," after Rahab the hospitable prostitute in the book of Joshua. Well-organized and planned, they gather now each Friday night at the church. They place lit candles in the low windows of the parish hall. They go out, two by two, and meet the women where they are, bars and street corners and parking lots. They invite them in for a bit of food, for some warmth. They keep a prayer space and a prayer-journal available for them. One volunteer stays behind and prays during the whole evening. A hired security guard stays in the parking lot to make sure that the women can come and go, unmolested by men, be they johns or pimps or what have you. They offer the women health information and supplies, referrals, clothing, and above all unconditional hospitality. It is a wonderful ministry, one of which I and the parish are deeply proud. A right-wing Episcopalian blogger and self-appointed watchdog of orthodoxy got hold of the ministry via the diocesan newspaper and excoriated it, misnaming it as "Rehab's Sisters" and claiming we condone prostitution in a typical act of liberal idiocy, failing to call the women to repentance "as did Jesus."

I think there is no higher compliment than that we be criticized for consorting, as it were, with prostitutes. Any flak we take for such a thing places us in good company, with the Lord himself, who was specifically suspect because he knew and spent time with the "working women." They are still getting into the Kingdom ahead of the modern-day Pharisees. That much hasn't changed. Now *there's* traditional Bible and orthodoxy for you! But comfortable theorists argue and gesticulate and quote and pontificate, and I am little better as I sit and write in a warm room. But still the candles are lit and the women go forth, and the women for whom the Lord had special love and care come in, through doors that they never darken on a Sunday morning. And who then is doing the will of the Father who is in heaven?

So that is the story of how Brigid's Mantle spread over a Northwest neighborhood. I wish I could give you a step-by-step process, a Celtic how-to book. For us it began with a dream and the wish to believe a dream. And it took shape when we looked about and saw, with eyes from which scales began to fall, who was really our neighbor, who is on our very doorstep. And we waited, with impatience, and asked over and over again "How?" and "Who?" And the answers came, in true quirky Celtic fashion, long silence punctuated with sudden insight and a tumble of released energy. And above all, when the gifts came, in people likely or unlikely, we welcomed them, we set a hearth and a home, "food in the eating place and music in the listening place." For as the old Irish poem assures, "Often, often goes the Christ in the stranger's guise." As I write, there is no sense that the story is done. My ears, if I try, hear the creak of taut fabric as Brigid's Mantle continues to stretch and be drawn over more land and lives than I can imagine. Perhaps I am the king of the old tale, who watches with shock and grudging admiration the full extent of what his agreement with Brigid has meant. But I am used to being ordered about by strong-willed Irish women and one who has been dead in the flesh for fifteen hundred years makes no particular exception. It is disconcerting. But it is also great fun.

chapter 22

companions
and culdees

T HE WRITING of a Rule of life seemed to be a natural step. Monastic life is an old phenomenon in the Church. It was the effort to
establish God's kingdom on earth, with the Christian Emperor as God's
vice-regent, that sent men and women flying to the deserts and away
from the centers of the "righteous empire" as from a shipwreck. So much
of history is cyclical. As we are in the midst of yet another manifestation
of "empire Christianity," it is no wonder that so many fly as did the Desert
Mothers and Fathers to what some are calling the "new monasticism,"
seeking communities of faith and integrity where the countercultural life
of the Gospel may be experienced.

Monastic life is nothing more than baptized Christian life writ large
and lived with daily passion and discipline, with God's help. Written
"Rules" and a community covenanted to mutual support and accountability are typical elements of the monastic tradition. It is at one and
the same time utterly ordinary and an impossible project. But with God,
all things are possible. Sometimes I think that I am only beginning to
believe that now.

Mary Stilwell, an active and committed parishioner, both encouraged
the formation of the Columba Center vision and was kindled by the
notion of re-imagined Celtic monasticism. It is due in large part to her
calm reflection and input that we composed and are living our two Rules.

The chief purpose of a Christian Rule is to have something to which
to return. Few if any of us need anything else to do, nor do we need
anything else to fail at. But a decent Rule always reminds us of what we

are called to, what makes our hearts kindle, and where our path lies. And it welcomes us back when we have strayed.

With time and much conversation with many, and looking at all manner of Rules ancient and modern, we composed the "Way of Columba." The word "rule" in our time runs the risk of conveying off-putting rigidity. We settled on "way" as it is dynamic and conveys the Celtic sense of *gyrovagus*, of ceaseless pilgrimage.

The eight aspects of the Way are:

1. Commitment to Christ

2. Common life (with one another, in small group, and in the parish community)

3. A life of prayer

4. Soul-friendship (the Celtic anamchara tradition which may involve formal spiritual direction, but is a non-professional and lay practice in its traditional form)

5. Accountability (to self, others, community, "time, talent, and treasure")

6. Service and witness for justice

7. Learning and study (theological as well as other forms of knowledge)

8. Pilgrim identity

Eleven of us first professed the Way on the first Sunday of Advent 2002. Since that time we have added to our number, by the grace of God, including one who is not a member of our own parish but lives her call and her ministry elsewhere, as well as Ellie, who is our "extern" Companion in Connecticut.

The experience of the Companions of Columba has not been an easy or simple thing. Without evaluation, accountability, and meaningful community, the Way risks being a mouthful of pieties or cheap grace. We began to try to offer a monthly meeting whereby those who came could share their life and journey and we could read and study a text together. Finally, four frazzled and dog-tired people, already up to our ears in church, sat blinking sleepily at one another suspecting that for health and family's sake we really should have been home. So we met and wrestled with the question: how best to form community, or support one another as we form community elsewhere? We've yet to have any clear answers. But the question is worth the wrestling. For it is a bigger question than just us. In a fragmented world, alienating and isolating, we long for community, something deeper, I think, than what is provided by the glow of our computer screens.

Mary wanted to live a "ramped up" version of the Way, perhaps eventually professing her vows before the bishop. And so together we wrote the Culdee Rule. Based on the Way of Columba, the Culdee is meant to be a "monk in the world," living a demanding regimen of prayer and devotion, of simplicity of life and service. The Culdee may be male or female, married or single. There is no monastery or convent — the Culdee is responsible for his or her own living. This also is the "old way" — the African desert monastics wove baskets and worked for the Nile farmers during the harvest.

Mary began a special period of formation. We used a wonderful resource allowing the Ignatian Spiritual Exercises to be adapted for someone leading an active life. Through the course of a year, Mary completed the Exercises and then helped mentor a second candidate. And now there are four Culdees, including myself, who professed the Culdee Rule for the first time on Ascension Day 2006.

We have been very transparent with two different bishops now, who had good questions and good counsel both. But after having inquired into the process of seeking official acknowledgment through the national Episcopal Church for the Companions and Culdees, we have placed that process on hold. I think we are not sure of gaining anything we do not already have. And perhaps we are far too new in this journey to be sure of what we want or are asking, or of what God wishes for us.

chapter 23

brigid's feast
and clothes and teeth

The great monastery of men and women presided over by Brigid of Kildare who, according to one ancient manuscript, was ordained a bishop, was a place of great abundance. For Brigid gave everything away. And so, it is said, God gave back even more to Brigid. So the poor flocked there, because there was always food in plenty. "To save every miserable man" was Herself's own avowed purpose. She once wished for "a lake of beer" to serve the King of Kings and the poor at a great banquet. Now that's my kind of saint.

When I arrived at Saints Peter and Paul, there was already a long-standing tradition of a hot meal program, served each Wednesday night to whoever comes. Some men and some women, some seniors and others on fixed income, the guests sit at tables and are served at place by volunteers. It felt natural to rename the program Brigid's Table when it was plain Brigid wanted a place in our common life. Diffusing the leadership into teams (first Wednesday and so on), as many as forty volunteers from the parish and many others from area churches come on a rotating basis and serve hot meals to thirty-five to fifty guests. Guests are led in prayer by volunteers who know their names and hear their pain and struggle, working it into vocal intercessions. The ministry has always been lay-led and lay-conducted.

Christianity makes so much more sense when one sits and talks with someone whose struggle makes one's own pale by comparison, and serves them and eats with them as well.

Many guests speak of the parish as "their church" and do a very firm job of calling one another to account for decent behavior and language on "holy ground."

The ministry has many miracles. But the greatest miracle is that we can all gather in one place and be human together, be at peace and serve one another. It is a healing place.

Part of the healing comes in the gift of serving. Metaphorical Celtic holes in the wall have been kicked that have allowed many people from the community to come and serve. Many newcomers to the parish begin active involvement by serving at Brigid's Table. Now some people find the parish by seeking out Brigid's Table and the chance to serve. Volunteers from two area churches and from a local Bible college, fellow students and Master Brown from Kim's Tae Kwon Do, and many others have come and continue to come. It's a messy but very loveable ministry, to paraphrase Archbishop Tutu. And it can be a place of miracles.

We always want to do more. There is so much more to do. Our new deacon feels strongly about establishing a regular practice of social services–type intake counseling. We have a long way to go, but generous donations ensure there are bus tickets and some $5 food tickets and emergency clothes in a closet.

And William Temple House, a venerable Episcopal-inspired social services agency downtown, has patiently pursued partnership with us. We finally hit upon a feasible project. William Temple has an arrangement with Northwest Medical Teams which provides a dental van, a dental clinic on wheels staffed by retired dentists. The parish vestry voted to put in a 220-volt electric line outside, a vestryman oversaw the installation, the diocese reimbursed the church for the cost, Mary Stilwell coordinated the schedule and the parish support volunteers, and now an impressive shiny van can be seen in the parking lot once or twice a month. Come too close and you can grit your teeth to the sound of a drill. But in a culture wherein medical and dental care is not a right but a purchased privilege, the van is always busy. Two or three would be just as busy, I'm sure. And Mary developed the ministry, inviting more church members to assist, conducting a back-to-school dental clinic for kids, and otherwise dreaming about reaching out to more.

One day, when the Reign of God is manifest in fullness, food and shelter and clothing and dignity and medical care will not be an inaccessible privilege, but a right. Then we'll have to find something else to do, or maybe take a rest. But meanwhile, we're having fun.

chapter 24

a push from shore

ONE OF THE MANY risks in writing this book is the temptation to think of it, to read it, as the marvels of one visionary fellow and the wonderful, wonderful things he has done with an army of selfless friends. But our urban Iona, if it proves to be over time a lasting vision, is no such thing. The paths were blazed long ago, in ancient Palestine around a new proclamation, in the cold seas around Ireland and Britain, on Iona's flinty rocks and thin soil, through the fields and fens and forests of Europe. And even then, all this would be one middle-aged white priest's conceit if a dream of a vivid and free and vibrant kind of faith-community had not found an echo and longing in many hearts, if it had not taken root amidst an already-existing community accustomed to story and sacrament and symbol, a community already experienced in ministering to the poor, a community hospitable and accustomed to hearing people's longing for the divine. And this vision has been supported and appropriated by many others who heard and have added their own stories and longings and have asked good hard questions, dug in and not expected anyone else to give them the answers, and have given their time and talent and treasure.

I am so very grateful. Let this book be one small way of saying "thank you." And thank you, pilgrim God, for being restlessness and road and companion and journey's end, all at once.

As I am sure I warned, this is not a book about ceaseless triumph, nor is it a book about a surefire way to double your church's size and answer the questions of faith and ministry that we all have to answer. Beware the glossy brochure that claims to do so! Recycle it along with all the other marketing mail that comes each day.

We wrestle daily. Brigid's Table is and always will be a challenging ministry as it calls many different types of people to work together, in a kitchen no less, and work kindly with a wounded population. But recently we were given several modest grants for remodeling of our kitchen as it is acknowledged as a place where the poor are served. With profoundly generous parishioner labor, as I write the kitchen has just been completed.

With the same generosity of spirit (and in many cases the same sets of generous hands), an outdoor labyrinth has been built and has become a quiet addition not only to church life, but a gift to the neighborhood as well.

Rahab's Sisters presents the same array of issues, and always invites the critique of those who find people in prostitution just too morally compromised and those who work with them too suspect to bear the brand-name of nice and righteous Christians. But the ministry has captured the imagination of many, has garnered some funding, and at this writing is the only organized form of outreach to sex workers, secular or religious, in the city of Portland. Considering the longstanding tradition of sex trade in this city, that fact makes us feel good but is chilling as well.

We the Companions and Culdees are still feeling our way, and as we are beginning to accept for profession Companions from other faith-communities the challenges of community and accountability will no doubt deepen before they will be resolved. We live in this and other questions, and we persevere, among other ministries, in sustaining daily noon "Office" or prayer in the church.

Mary Stilwell had been titled "prior" and a valiant, devoted group of energized women have worked with us to find funding for her half-time stipend. But we're always broke and had been barely scraping her package together until recently, when we finally came to the bottom of our barrel. We've received a number of small grants, and have been refused a couple of big ones. A small number of generous folks have been helping us through private donations.

One of the original Companions was just ordained a deacon, and has addressed our vision with new energy. We have taught classes to the larger community ranging from Celtic Christian spirituality to theological themes in Tolkien's *Lord of the Rings*, and each time we find people eager to hear of our next adventure and what we may have to say in the meanwhile. We're working to take over a local academy of theological education, the Metro-East School of Ministry. And we've met and made great new friends outside of our small circles. Our community is larger than us, and our borders have indeed become more porous.

We usually get just what we need and no more.

But we have shoved off from shore on this voyage, and have learned to navigate choppy seas and to enjoy the winds even when they blow from unexpected quarters. And it seems that everywhere we hear echoes and similar cries for authentic community and a passionate following of Christ, one not trammeled by old structures that have become the "old wineskins" of the Gospels. We've been deeply drawn by the so-called "Emerging Church" movement, and feel kinship with this energy to form new kinds of community which speak openly of new ways to live ancient faith and even "new monasticism." In our attempts to ask the hard questions that we believe the Gospel asks, in our hunger for God and to serve the servant Christ, perhaps we are part of something much larger, a new wind blowing through old structures and old, weary communities. We talk with an ever-widening circle of people these days, and find more and more kindred hearts.

For all my middle age, I feel young, younger than I have in years. It's just harder to get going in the morning. I do not know if this is a "true" vision of life. Perhaps that is not the right question to ask. At least it is a vision. And a vision is a worthwhile thing to have in an age of dogmatism, violence, idolatry, and despair.

Old Abba, tough old warrior from Kerry, island soldier Columba, do you sit still on your crag, staring across the sound to where the pilgrims waved their arms to signal the ferry-boat? Did you come across the sea, and do you sit on our mossy peaked roof on 82nd Avenue, greeting pilgrims again? You said, I am sure, that a vision would be given, but that we'd have to work for it. Pray that our work not be wasted, pray that we be honest in our seeking and our searching. Pray that, as you prayed at the end, there be at least a small door left open for us into the endless feasting-hall.

Appendix A

A VISION
"the columba center:
prayer, reflection, action"

Description

A parish-based resource for spiritual formation, Christian reflection, and direct service and action on behalf of those in physical, financial, spiritual need. Ecumenical and involving the participation and sponsorship of eastside Episcopal parishes, as well as interested congregations of other denominations, as well as area agencies.

Rationale

St. Columba founded on Iona a thriving monastic community centered in prayer and study, yet fostering the arts and offering both hospitality and service to the poor as well as evangelizing mission to Scotland and northern England. Tiny, barren Iona became known as the "Rome of the North," fostering Christian learning and spiritual life, "spinning off" other communities throughout Great Britain and Europe.

SS. Peter and Paul is an Episcopal parish rooted in the Anglo-Catholic tradition. An essential component part of the Anglo-Catholic revival of the nineteenth century was what became known as the "Social Gospel," placing the preaching of the Kingdom to the poor into action in the working-class slums of England, feeding bodies, preaching to souls, supporting the working class in their cry for justice.

The rich spirit of Columba and Brigid and other Celtic saints fits well with SS. Peter and Paul's rich sense of the presence and experience of God, sense of outreach, concern for justice and for the poor, and love and concern for the natural world as evidenced in our care for our wooded grounds amidst the commercial landscape of 82nd Avenue.

SS. Peter and Paul, through the change of roadways and neighborhood over the years, is among all parishes of the Diocese uniquely poised on an urban outpost, a major roadway and conduit for transients, the poor, and persons in prostitution. SS. Peter and Paul is also poised, through slow but steady numerical growth, young and energetic people in leadership, a sense of search for vision, and the successful but incomplete Capital Funds Drive, for a Spirit-filled challenge that will make a future for the parish based on mission and not survival.

Components

- Brigid's Table meal ministry (already in place one night/week, administered by parishioners)
- teaching opportunities in Bible, Christian social reflection, and spirituality (now offered through parish ministries, primarily for parishioners). Some examples of potential topics: daily living with Scripture; Christian views on poverty and economics; ecumenical and interfaith conversation; "Prayer of the Heart" and contemplative traditions; Anglican Rosary; Labyrinth; storytelling as spiritual praxis; poetry as spiritual search; leadership and Baptismal ministry; St. Francis and Franciscan spirituality; Celtic spirituality. Many of these already have been offered by parish clergy and lay members.
- food pantry
- trained referral counselors (volunteer), with bus fare and meal tickets available, as well as an emergency clothes closet
- outreach and counseling for persons in prostitution, with eventual foundation of long-term residential rehab program for women getting out of "the life" (off-site location)
- group work in life skills, job search for homeless/unemployed
- one or more 12-Step groups
- spiritual care available to walk-ins, prayer and possible healing ministry
- internship offered to Diocesan diaconal candidates

- a "cell" or "desert," a private retreat room, available through arrangement with the Rector, for personal prayer, with spiritual direction available by prearrangement
- possible foundation of a residential or nonresidential religious community, inspired by Celtic monastic tradition, open to men and women, who would pray for and possibly serve in Columba Center's ministries.

Requirements and Resources

- Vestry and parish of SS. Peter and Paul "buying into" the vision; ownership and willingness to work and lead
- talents and gifts of individual parishioners regarding outreach, spirituality, organization, planning, physical plant, grant writing
- successful completion of Capital Funds drive so that long-term changes in physical plant may be planned with Center in mind
- support of National Church with Jubilee Center status sought
- support of Diocese through acknowledgement, grants
- some linkage with William Temple House and networking of resources for social service and outreach
- support and possible co-sponsorship by Metro-East Episcopal parishes, ecumenical partnership sought through Montavilla churches. Volunteers, organizational gifts, publicity all sought
- linkage with Diocesan School for the Diaconate
- guest faculty for teaching from Diocese, other ecumenical sources
- Montavilla Neighborhood Association, URS Club contact.

Timeline

Classes/spiritual services offered within one year's time, food pantry and referral resources ditto, expanded physical plant for office, storage, meeting and teaching space (which also includes improved office, church school, nursery, fellowship space for the parish) in five to ten years.

Spring 2002

appendix b

"way of the culdee"
draft amplified rule of life
for culdees of the columba center

This draft Rule is an amplification of aspect #2 of the Commentary on the "Way of Columba," that there may be "those who feel drawn to make formal vows to the Way, living it with an advanced degree of observance. Such folk are to be supported and offered the careful discernment of the leadership and Companions, consulting the local Bishop and other church authorities when appropriate" (*Commentary*, 4).

Within the history of Celtic monasticism, a renewal movement began in the eighth century which sought to return to the rigor and passion of the early age of the Celtic Church, the "age of saints" of the fourth to sixth centuries. Including within it the monastery of Tallagh and its great abbot Maelruain, adherents of the movement called themselves "Celi De," "clients of God" or "friends of God," later rendered as "Culdees." Sometimes living as solitaries alone or appended onto residential communities, sometimes on constant pilgrimage as "gyrovagus," sometimes comprising whole communities, the Culdees were living examples of a fervent and intentional life consecrated to Christ, and by example were a force for renewal within the whole Celtic Church.

The modern vocation of Culdee is meant to be just such a presence within the Columba Center, parish life, and the larger church. Drawing on the Celtic monastic heritage, those who (after careful discernment and a probationary period) vow themselves as Culdees will live an amplification and intensification of the "Way of Columba." Accountable to both the Abba of the Columba Center as well as to the local bishop or bishop's delegate, the Culdee will make of their own lives the "peregrinatio Cristi," the "pilgrimage of Christ," and will serve as witness and leaven for the larger Church.

The following amplification assumes that the Culdee will continue to observe all of the other demands of the "Way of Columba" and its Commentary:

1. Commitment to Christ

The Culdee will seek to immerse her/himself in the mystery of Christ through. . . .

a. Word: the Culdee will engage in ongoing study of the four canonical Gospels, alone, with a tutor, in a small-group setting, or in a formal class. The goal of this is not intellectual knowledge so much as the nurture of a warm and living love of Christ and a further exploration of the mystery of Christ as presented in Scripture. Study of the whole Bible, as well as of the early Church Fathers and Mothers, is also highly encouraged.

b. Sacrament: the Culdee will affiliate with a parish community in which the celebration of the Eucharist occupies a central place. The Culdee will attend Eucharist and communicate on the Sundays of the year as well as on all major feasts when possible.

c. Service: the Culdee will make time for some form of "hands-on" ministry to the poor and needy. At the Columba Center's site of SS. Peter and Paul, Brigid's Table meal program, Rahab's Sisters ministry to persons in prostitution, and other present and future servant ministries provide excellent opportunities for this. The Culdee is to be open to other opportunities, especially if he/she lives near and worships at a place other than SS. Peter and Paul.

2. Common Life

The Culdee will seek or create, whenever possible, a "muintir" or small group setting where a real shared life in Christ may be lived. Such small group communities may change or come and go as time goes on.

The life of the Culdee is not meant to be restricted to one specific state of life. The Culdee may discern that she/he is called upon to live as a solitary, or as a member of a family, or in intentional community with others called to the same way of life. In any case, the Culdee is to strive to form authentic Christian community with those whom she/he is called to live, a life based on prayer, hospitality, service, and love in charity. A first step in living Common Life is naming and declaring blessed those communities of which the Culdee is already part, whether familial, professional, or intentional, and infusing their life together with Celtic Christian values.

3. A Life of Prayer

a. The Culdee will pray a full Daily Office. The Daily Office of the Episcopal Book of Common Prayer is recommended as it makes use of the whole Psalter (a central feature of Celtic Christian devotion) and includes a lectionary or schedule for course reading of the Bible. Other forms of Daily Office such as *Celebrating Common Prayer, Celtic Prayers From Iona, A Northumbrian Daily Office* or other Celtic forms, resources from Lutheran, Roman Catholic, ecumenical communities such as that of Taizé, or other sources could also be used. The Abba or Prior could assist the Culdee in choosing a form of Office. The exact form is not of primary importance. It is simply important to have an Office, a regular daily rhythm of praise of God, listening to God, and praying to God in Christ, firmly rooted in the Scriptures. Daily Morning and Evening Prayer are the standard required of a serious daily Office. Midday Prayer and Night Prayer are also encouraged. It is highly recommended that the Culdee pause for intentional prayer at or near noon so as to join in spirit with the Office offered by the Companions of Columba at SS. Peter and Paul. Prayer upon retiring may take the form of a formal Compline or night prayer drawn from the BCP or other sources, or may take the form of an Ignatian "examination of conscience." It is highly recommended that the Daily Office be enriched by Canticles, Collects, and other prayers drawn from Celtic sources. The Abba and Prior can suggest or make available resources for these. One of the Daily Offices should always include the prayer "Kindle in our hearts, O God..." attributed to St. Columba. The Canticle "Columba's Rock" is highly recommended for use on Thursdays.

b. The Culdee shall also devote one hour daily to private prayer. This may be done in one sitting, or broken into two half-hour periods, or further broken throughout the day as circumstances demand. The form of prayer pursued during this time would be left to the discretion of the Culdee, drawing freely from the riches of Christian tradition when helpful. The Holy Spirit can be trusted to guide the Culdee in how to pray aright, and it is assumed that the "anamchara" or soul-friend of the Culdee, as well as the Abba, will be of help in exploring the rich heritage of Christian spirituality.

c. The Culdee shall practice intercessory prayer as an essential part of her/his vocation, and shall pray for those in need. The Culdee shall pray for the Columba Center, the parish, the diocesan Bishop, for world peace and repentance from the ways of violence and power, and for the poor and the oppressed.

d. The Culdee shall participate actively in the worship life of the Church, paying special attention to the celebration of the Eucharist. The Culdee is encouraged to take active roles in the liturgy at the discretion of the priest or pastor.

e. The Culdee shall practice Reconciliation and seek to live a reconciled life, accepting the free gift of the mercy of God and living at shalom with others. The Culdee is encouraged to make confession at least once a year to a member of the clergy. If one is not available or if the practice of oral confession presents too many stumbling blocks, the Culdee is encouraged to celebrate reconciliation regularly with an *anamchara* or another trusted Christian. Remember that the form for Reconciliation in the Episcopal Book of Common Prayer provides for a "Declaration of Forgiveness" to be offered by a layperson.

The Culdee shall seek to be a reconciling presence in the world, courageously witnessing to the Prince of Peace at all times.

f. The Culdee shall maintain a practice of "spiritual reading," always "keeping a book going" which is chosen for its capacity to feed the spirit and support the Christian journey of the Culdee. Special attention should be given to the Sayings of the Desert Fathers and Mothers as well as early Celtic monastic sources.

g. The Culdee shall observe the feasts of St. Brigid (February 1), St. Patrick (March 17), and St. Columba (June 9) with special joy, attending Eucharist or otherwise celebrating the feasts with intentional prayer and festivity. Observance of other Celtic feast days is highly encouraged.

   Thursdays are always Columba's Day in accord with Celtic monastic practice, unless superseded by other feasts. The day's Office is appropriately supplemented with the canticle "Columba's Rock" or material from Columba's "Altus Prosator," and the Collect from St. Columba's Day may appropriately be used. Thursdays are also especially appropriate days to pray the Office with others or to attend the Eucharist.

h. The Culdee shall observe a monthly "desert day" in which she/he will withdraw from all normal work, ministry, or other activities insofar as is possible. This day may be spent at home, if the atmosphere allows for such disengagement, or may be spent at another location. The day shall be spent in silence and solitude insofar as is possible, and only the Scriptures shall be used as reading matter.

i. The ancient Celtic Church observed three Lents, and St. Benedict as well described the life of the monastic as "a continuous Lent" (*Rule of Benedict* 49:1). Although literal imitation of the early Fathers and Mothers is probably not advisable, the Culdee shall honor the spirit of the penitential heritage of the Celtic Church, by which each was called to continual conversion of life, by honoring the tradition of fasting. These are some ways to do so:

   1. The Culdee is invited to observe a Western church-fast (one full meal without excess, two further servings which together

do not comprise one full meal) on two select weekdays, excluding Sunday, during the after-Pentecost season until 1 Advent, and from Epiphany to Ash Wednesday. Wednesdays and Fridays are traditional days on which to so do, but other days may be chosen as circumstances dictate.

2. The Culdee may observe the same church-fast on all the weekdays of Lent and Advent, excluding Saturdays and Sundays.

3. Fasting is forbidden on Sundays, during all the days of Eastertide and Christmastide, on all feast of the Lord and other major feasts, and on the feasts of SS. Brigid, Patrick, or Columba.

4. There are many reasons in Christian tradition for fasting. One honored reason is fasting in solidarity with those who suffer hunger or injustice. Such fasting may be undertaken with a larger call to fast in regard to a particular cause or event. Another form of fasting in solidarity is to do so in union with sisters and brothers of other faiths. The Culdee may consider fasting in solidarity on the Jewish Day of Atonement (Yom Kippur) or during the Muslim fasting month of Ramadan, during which nothing is taken by mouth from sunup to sundown. In each case inter-religious reconciliation through personal discipline is being expressed.

5. Any fasting in excess of this is only to be undertaken in consultation with the Abba and the anamchara of the Culdee, and for a proscribed length of time. It is to be remembered that fasting is a tool and aid, never a goal, and is to be mitigated or discontinued whenever it seems to threaten physical, mental, or spiritual health.

j. The Culdee shall make an annual retreat of at least five days insofar as is possible. This retreat may be directed or simply a time spent in silence and recollection. If need be, the Culdee may make this retreat while living at home or working, in a manner similar to the conduct of the "19th Annotation" of the Ignatian Exercises.

4. Soul-friendship

The Culdee shall have an "anamchara" or spiritual friend, and shall cultivate this friendship regularly. The tradition of "spiritual director" nurtured in the Western church may be one way to fulfill this ministry. But the gift and ministry of anamchara is the older tradition in the Celtic lands, and may prove to be more accessible as it is non-professionalized.

The Culdee shall be open to being an "anamchara" to others, and shall engage in such relationships with a full heart but with discretion, consulting the Abba or her/his own anamchara if any issues or concerns arise.

5. Accountability

a. The life that the Culdee undertakes is a serious one, and the witness to the larger Church and world is a calling, a grace, and a responsibility. Hence the Culdee is a person in a stance of listening to the promptings of the Spirit in private discernment, in the counsel of their anamchara, the role of the Abba, the authority of the local Bishop and other church officers, and the life of the larger Church.

b. The Culdee is to remain aware that all things spring forth from God and are to be given back to God joyfully. The Culdee shall embrace the tithe as the minimum standard of Christian giving, and shall tithe to the local congregation where the Culdee has taken spiritual root. A donation to the life and ministry of the Columba Center shall also be given. The Culdee shall make an annual financial accounting of her/his affairs to the Abba or Prior, who shall hold the information in confidence.

c. The Culdee is not vowed to celibacy by her/his profession, and is free to be open to the relationships placed in her/his life. The Culdee is to observe Christian chastity according to her/his state of life, remaining aware of the many temptations to exploitation in our time and culture. The Culdee is free to marry, informing both the Abba and the Bishop beforehand. If the Culdee intends to embrace lifelong celibacy, she/he may do so and vow to do so, but only after careful discernment and consultation with the Abba and Bishop.

d. The Culdee is to make quarterly visits to the Abba or Prior in order to make account of her/his observance of the rule in general, and is to write an annual letter to the Bishop in the spirit of "manifestation of conscience," telling the Bishop of the joys, sorrows, and challenges of the life undertaken.

e. In case of conflict regarding the interpretation and living of the Rule, the Culdee shall work together with the Abba and Prior as well as the other Culdees, consulting at need the Bishop and work with him/her or a person that the Bishop appoints.

6. Service and Witness for Justice

The Culdee shall regard deep awareness of the real-life sorrows, joys, and struggles of the world as intrinsic to her/his calling. The Culdee shall pray for a more just world, seek to raise her/his consciousness of the struggle of the poor, the marginalized, and the oppressed, and seek ways in which she/he may actively work on behalf of justice. Christ may be encountered on a picket line or in a congressman's office as readily as he may be in prayer.

7. Learning and Study

a. The Culdee shall value learning, and shall engage in ongoing biblical study as well as the study of the history of religious life, the Celtic Church, and other related areas, with the help and consultation of the Abba.

b. The Culdee shall be open to further theological education, in the forms of formal divinity studies, EFM, other approved programs, or individual reading and study.

c. The Culdee shall also value ongoing learning and formation in other fields, remembering the love for and valuing of the life of the mind that was the hallmark of the Celtic saints and monastics. Ongoing educational goals shall be part of the accountability rendered quarterly and annually by the Culdee.

8. *Pilgrim Identity*

a. The Culdee shall actively seek at least one opportunity in her/his lifetime to go on pilgrimage to the British Isles, visiting prayerful holy sites such as Iona, Lindisfarne, Kildare, Glendalough, and others.

b. The Culdee shall remember that he/she is a pilgrim on earth, and will seek ways to "tread lightly," remembering that the true home of the Christian is in Christ.

c. The Culdee shall observe simplicity in her/his use of the world's good, remembering that the life of a religious is meant to mirror the truth that true happiness is found in Christ, as well as the fact that most of the world lives in hunger and want in order that the privileged may live in luxury. Excessive accumulation or consumption is antithetical to the life and witness of the Culdee.

d. The Culdee shall write a will disposing all of her/his earthly possessions, remembering the local congregation and the Columba Center in the bequest.

annotateð bibliography
of celtic christian
anð relateð sources

Look up "Celtic" or "Celtic Christian" online or at your library, and get thoroughly intimidated by the tidal wave of results. I am sure I've only scratched the surface. But here are some books that I have grown to love or that helped to form my own pilgrimage. As a result, they still do.

Adomnan of Iona. *Life of Saint Columba.* Richard Sharpe, trans. London: Penguin Books, 1995. Adomnan wrote only a century after the death of the Abbot-founder while Adomnan himself served as the Abbot of Iona. Indispensable reading for Columba-heads, Adomnan gives insight into the inner workings of the ancient Iona community as well as the saint himself. The introduction is worth reading in itself as an overview of early Celtic monasticism. Of course, the best way to read Adomnan is seated on a crag on Iona, facing the sea. . . .

Bradley, Ian. *Celtic Christian Communities: Live the Tradition.* Kelowna, British Columbia: Northstone Publishing, 2000. Bradley is a prominent writer in the current Celtic Christian revival, and a scholarly and honest one. He followed his first enthusiastic book with one of scholarly penitence, *Celtic Christianity: Making Myths and Chasing Dreams.* I trust Bradley having read how he deconstructs the romantic mythologizing that has characterized each revival of interest in the Celtic Christians, including the current one. This book describes several elements of the early Celtic Christians worthy and practical to recover today, including the formation of community and the ancient practice and spirituality of pilgrimage.

Clancy, Padraigin, ed. *Celtic Threads: Exploring the Wisdom of Our Heritage.* Dublin: Veritas Publications, 1999. A great anthology of reflections and research by modern Irish/Celtic folks "on the ground" who are living the tradition that they seek to uncover and recover for today. A few of these folks appear in my own book (Sr. Mary Minehan, Michael Rodgers, Marcus Losack).

Clancy, Thomas Owen and Gilbert Markus, ed. and trans. *Iona: The Earliest Poetry of a Celtic Monastery.* Edinburgh: University of Edinburgh Press, 1995. It's essential to go to primary-source material if one wants to avoid floating wholly away on Celtic mists. This wonderful and not-easy-to-find collection of ancient Latin and Gaelic poetry and prayer gives a clear sense of the sturdy and unsentimental spirituality of Iona in its early days. The translator-editors are wonderful scholars, but their preface, albeit solid historically, sometimes reflects a somewhat sour established-church backlash against the recovery of the Celtic Christian narrative.

Cousineau, Phil. *The Art of Pilgrimage: The Seeker's Guide to Making Travel Sacred.* Berkeley, CA: Conari Press, 1998. An odd partner to the above book is this wondrous and utterly cross-traditional guide for anyone seeking the Holy and feeling their feet itch as they do so. On my list of things to do before I die is to just go somewhere with Phil Cousineau and learn how he walks as a pilgrim no matter where the destination. I'm picky about the books I keep on my shelves; this is one I'll only lend for short periods of time.

Davies, Oliver, trans. *Celtic Spirituality.* The Classics of Western Spirituality Series. New York: Paulist Press, 1999. An indispensable anthology of Celtic primary-source material, as fine as the other volumes in the series. Of special interest to the Celtophile is some material of the often-maligned Pelagius, and the sermon by John Scotus Eriugena where he makes the case of the Celtic Christians being the "church of Saint John" who "listen to the heartbeat of God."

Doherty, Jerry C. *A Celtic Model of Ministry: The Reawakening of Community Spirituality.* Collegeville, MN: The Liturgical Press, 2003. Doherty is an Episcopal priest whose Celtic reflections are based in actual practice as rector of a large congregation. I like especially his notes about "authentic community" and his speaking of the need for a Rule of life for all congregational members.

Merton, Thomas, trans. *The Wisdom of the Desert.* New York: New Directions, 1970. The late Thomas Merton did much to rescue the Desert Fathers and Mothers from scholarly church obscurity with this select translation of Sayings with a long introduction. A good source for getting a taste of the seminal Desert tradition, before tackling longer collections of the Sayings and the Lives.

Moorhouse, Geoffrey. *Sun Dancing: A Vision of Medieval Ireland.* New York: Harcourt, Brace, and Co., 1997. Moorhouse is both an historian and a writer of fiction. This work succeeds both in giving fascinating archaeological and historical information about Skellig Michael, the desert-style monastery perched impossibly on a big rock off of Ireland's southwest coast, while fictionalizing several different moments in its 600–year history. Skellig Michael was in many ways Extreme Celtic Monasticism and may not have been "typical," but in other ways shared completely in the spiritual roots and culture of Celtic monastic houses.

Newell, J. Philip. *Celtic Prayers from Iona.* Mahwah, NJ: Paulist Press, 1997. Newell is a former Warden of The Iona Community and a gifted writer in his own right. There are many books of Celtic prayers, either translations or contemporary works Celtic-inspired. Newell's genius lies in his immersion in the Hebridean folk prayer tradition gathered by Alexander Carmichael, the prayers usually considered "Celtic" by most folks, and working them into a usable form for twice-daily prayer. The Companions of Columba use the book as our midday Office book at the church. The book includes a one-year table for reading the Gospels and Psalms.

O'Duinn, Sean. *Where Three Streams Meet: Celtic Spirituality.* Blackrock, Ireland: The Columba Press, 2000. A Benedictine monk and scholar, O'Duinn has a refreshingly original way of exploring the native Celtic tradition. He speaks of concepts and themes I have rarely found elsewhere, including the concept of *neart* or innate divine energy, as well as folk customs such as the keening and the confluence of ancient Celtic fire-feasts (Samhainn, Beltane etc.) and Christian folk custom.

O Maidin, Uinseann. *The Celtic Monk: Rules and Writings of Early Irish Monks.* Kalamazoo, MI: Cistercian Publications, 1996. A unique collection and translation of early Irish monastic rules, readable and including some poetry and prayers. Beautiful photos of ruins and High Crosses help place the rules in context.

Robson, Pat. *A Celtic Liturgy.* London: HarperCollins, 2000. Robson is an Anglican priest ministering in Wales amidst that manifestation of the Celtic church. This is an elegantly presented small hardback, the contents of which beautifully blends contemporary Celtic-inspired texts with translations of ancient material. Some of the contemporary material is the author's own graceful poetry.

Rodgers, Michael, and Marcus Losack. *Glendalough: A Celtic Pilgrimage.* Harrisburg, PA: Morehouse Publishing, 1996. The ultimate pilgrim's guide to Glendalough, the book makes possible an "armchair pilgrimage" and is well worth the reading even if you never stand in the car-park and listen to the cleaning man mutter about the "first suckers of the day."

Sheldrake, Philip. *Living Between Worlds: Place and Journey in Celtic Spirituality.* Cambridge, MA: Cowley Publications, 1995. A scholarly work, Sheldrake eloquently speaks of the role of borders and boundaries in classical Celtic consciousness and how they are reflected in ancient Celtic art and architecture. His concluding chapter on Iona functions as a good pilgrim's introduction to the island.

Van Der Weyer, Robert. *Celtic Gifts: Orders of Ministry in the Celtic Church.* Norwich, CT: Canterbury Press, 1997. A provocative work of fiction, this little book has stirred up some creative imagination while functioning as a good introduction to a re-imagined Celtic Christian spirituality. Bishop Ladehoff had all us clergy read the book back in the 1990s, and it stirred up energies that are reverberating today. An English bishop reorients the life of his diocese along re-imagined Celtic lines, with surprising results.